P15-008

Changing Styles in Shakespeare

Changing Styles in Shakespeare

RALPH BERRY

London
GEORGE ALLEN & UNWIN
Boston   Sydney

First published in 1981

GEORGE ALLEN & UNWIN LTD
40 Museum Street, London WC1A 1LU

© George Allen & Unwin (Publishers) Ltd, 1981

British Library Cataloguing in Publication Data

Berry, Ralph
    Changing styles in Shakespeare.
    1. Shakespeare, William – Stage history
    I. Title
    792.9   PR3091

    ISBN 0-04-822042-6

Set in 10 on 11½ point Plantin by Alan Sutton, Gloucester
and printed in Great Britain
by A. Wheaton & Co., Exeter.

Contents

Acknowledgements	*page*	x
Introduction		1
1 The Metamorphoses of *Coriolanus*		18
2 *Measure for Measure*		37
3 *Troilus and Cressida*		49
4 *Henry V*		67
5 *Hamlet*		84
6 The Season of *Twelfth Night*		109
Index		120

For Frances

Acknowledgements

I am glad to acknowledge the help given by the Canada Council, which granted me a Leave Fellowship to work on this project. Portions of this book have appeared in *New York Literary Forum*, *Humanities Association Review* and *Shakespeare Quarterly:* I am indebted to the editors of those journals for permission to reprint. And finally I should like to acknowledge the courtesy and help given to me by Miss Molly Sole, Clerk to the Governors of the Old Vic and by the librarians of the Shakespeare Centre Library and the Folger Shakespeare Library.

Introduction

This book is a study of some ways in which Shakespeare has changed on the contemporary stage, in essence in England. It is not a work of stage history: that implies a fullness of commitment to the past, and to all matters that the stage embraces, that I cannot pretend to. Nor is it devoted to the Shakespeare canon as a whole – an impossibly wide undertaking. Nor, even within the limits of a few plays, can it hope to cover all the major productions within a single national frontier. Selectivity is imposed upon me by the nature of the inquiry. My focus is on the contemporary stage, in England, and my aim is to describe something for which the stage is a working model: our changing perception of Shakespeare, and the ways in which we have refashioned Shakespeare after our own image.

Shakespeare changes incessantly, for the sufficient reason that we change. His texts contain more *information* than those of any other dramatist, and are infinitely susceptible to reinterpretation. In choosing one of his dramas, a director reanimates it with the spirit of his own society and day. In addition to his personal vision, he will identify some current social assumptions and preoccupations in his production. He has no choice. So the history of Shakespearean productions is always a guide of sorts to the times. But this banal statement is true of all plays, in all eras. And not all of Shakespeare's plays pose equally interesting challenges. One could meditate profitably on the scene from *The Two Gentlemen of Verona* that Holman Hunt painted, and compare it with its descendant on today's stage. One could relate the gestures of Garrick's Richard III, as painted by William Hogarth, to Olivier's. Something of value is always to be gleaned from these transformations of cultural history. Still, I have preferred to concentrate on those plays which seem to me to offer a sharper and more intense challenge, and especially those plays whose provisional meaning has shifted very noticeably of late years.

For not all plays change greatly. If we could converse with a mid-Victorian playgoer about his and our *Macbeth*, there would be no great problem of discourse. He would be interested to find our Lady Macbeths younger, more attractive. We could converse knowledgeably on the advisability of a Scottish accent for Macbeth. There would naturally be matters of stage lighting, costume, and other technical refinements of presentation that separate our *Macbeth* from his.[1] But, differences of idiom aside, there would be no doubt that we were discussing the same play. *Macbeth* is the story of a basically moral human being, who commits an atrocious crime to further his ambitions, and is destroyed by the Fates and his own conscience. Nothing can change that fundamental proposition, that statement of the play's basic nature. And I dare say that our mid-Victorian would share, broadly, our sense of *Richard III*, or *Julius Caesar*, or *Love's Labour's Lost*. But with other texts the gulf in approach would widen. How could we discuss *Coriolanus*, if that play is held to be about a noble though somewhat stiff-necked Roman rightly rebuking the mob for unworthy behaviour? How discuss *Henry V*, if it is nothing but a celebration of a deserved triumph over the French? As for *Measure for Measure*, I can scarcely conceive of a dialogue here. Today's adverse treatment of the Duke would seem a perversity, almost a blasphemy, to our Victorian. He would have serious difficulties in concluding that we were discussing the same play.

Some plays change radically, while others simply keep pace with the organic movement of society and do little more than reflect changes of idiom and style. All plays respond to the movement of history, and to the accumulation of knowledge and experience it implies. With some – *Othello*, say, or *Richard III* – this movement tends to extend and confirm what we already know. We are better informed about the psychology of racial alienation, and of compensatory impulses stemming from physical inadequacies. With others – *The Tempest*, *Measure for Measure*, perhaps *King Lear* – the accretions to our knowledge affect profoundly our perception of the play. There is in this no rule that I can discover. It is partly a matter of the play's essence, partly of history and of social cognition.

By 'social cognition' I mean the capacity of a given society, in its day, to recognise the permanent truths that are coded into a Shakespeare text. I have in this no theory of social progress, though I am sure that some, at least, of the barbarisms recorded in the stage history of Shakespeare will not be repeated in the future. And I think it must broadly be true that we now can see better Shakespeare on stage than our ancestors could – performances more intelligently conceived and mounted, more sensitively acted.[2] But this does not necessarily mean that we always see more of the play's truth than our ancestors did. I think, rather, that each era is capable of perceiving certain areas of the truth, and that it perceives what is there in the play. The shaft of light falls through space, and particles of dust are clearly visible within it; beyond, not. Time moves, and the angle of incidence of the light shifts; the audience perceives a different kind of truth, which may supplement or displace the earlier. This change easily accommodates itself to the counterstatement that is always available concerning a major Shakespearean character – a concept well understood since Morgann's remarks on Falstaff. For instance, Shylock is a study of a man consumed by hate. There is none the less a subtly supportive account of the man, which explains him as reacting to alien stereotypes and as revenging himself upon the cruelties of Venetian society. The case for Shylock, as made by Olivier in Jonathan Miller's remarkable production for the National Theatre, 1970 (admittedly with the aid of a cut soliloquy: I, iii, 42–53), expands the sympathetic understanding of him latent in the text. Conversely, Brutus' obsession with his 'honour' has been scrutinized sceptically, notably in John Wood's performance for Trevor Nunn's *Julius Caesar* (1972). The man need not be taken at his own estimate. This revaluation of character – and, thus, of the entire play – is a central possibility in all of Shakespeare's plays, and goes far towards meeting, and co-operating with, a changed social perception.[3]

For a fuller explanation, we have to go beyond the theatre, and seek an account of English social life; and that is well beyond my scope. Since the focus of this book is on the postwar era, however, it does seem desirable to identify at least the major phases of this period. Two major studies by Bernard Levin and Christopher Booker[4] concur in regarding the 1960s as a self-contained and highly individual era, sharply separated from the values of the immediate postwar years and the 1970s. Booker, more interestingly, seeks to identify the point at which the 'sixties' became at least retrospectively visible:

> Anyone who looks at the evolution of English social history over the twenty years following the Second World War must be struck by the profound change that took place in and around the year 1956.[5]

The year 1956, the *annus mirabilis* of Suez and Hungary, is to theatre historians a peculiarly resonant date: it marks the première of Osborne's *Look Back in Anger*. However much they fret at the cliché, theatre historians concur with John Elsom that '*Look Back in Anger* came to symbolize the urgent demand for change'.[6] The abrupt change of climate is epitomized by Terence Rattigan, who recalled wryly:

There I was in 1956, a reasonably successful playwright with *Separate Tables* just opened, and suddenly the whole Royal Court thing exploded and Coward and Priestley and I were all dismissed, sacked by the critics.[7]

As for the sixties, there would, I imagine, be general agreement that 1968, the year of the student riots and the conclusion to Johnson's presidency, signalled the end of an era. This, too, is a date useful to the theatre historian, for Peter Hall resigned from the directorship of the Royal Shakespeare Company, a position he had held since 1960. The RSC, of all theatres, has had incomparably the greatest influence on the contemporary reception of Shakespeare. Hall's successor, Trevor Nunn, has made no great changes in RSC policy, but his subtle modifications of the existing style symbolize the evolution of a new decade. One does not apply a grid to time, but it will generally be useful to the reader to bear in mind the three phases of contemporary theatre life: 1945–56, postwar; 1956–68, 'the sixties'; 1968 onwards, the present.

Shakespeare on stage is a product of the commerce between academics and theatre people. This relationship is immensely complex, dynamic, and subtle, not lending itself to clear generalizations. Nevertheless, a few points can be made. Stage and academe are closer today than ever before. 'There was a time – a pre-Sprague era – when the worlds of the study and the stage seemed to be separated by an almost unbridgeable chasm.'[8] All that has changed. The leading directors fill their programmes with citations from the critics they are currently backing; it is naturally arguable whether critics influence directors, or whether directors choose which critics are to be rescued or, at any rate, shielded from obscurity. The directors themselves are men of academic standing. Peter Hall, Jonathan Miller, Trevor Nunn and John Barton are all Cambridge men (Barton was a don there); Peter Brook is Oxford, Terry Hands Birmingham. On the academic side, an awareness of performance values is increasingly regarded as essential to first-rate criticism. Alexander Leggatt's *Shakespeare's Comedy of Love* (1974) – in substance, a work of impeccable academic scholarship – quotes freely from recent productions, as illustrations of textual points considered by the writer. A growing number of academics are engaged actively with theatre, as actors, directors, reviewers, even dramaturges. The view of Shakespeare's text as a set of stage directions, as a design for performance, increasingly commends itself to academics.

The interpenetration of stage and academe makes it hard to

distinguish the contribution of each. And yet the values and imperatives of the two worlds are very different. Theatre people are much more closely in touch with the public than scholars are, in their professional existence. If an academic publishes a banal or passé account of a play, it will encounter at worst some review hostility, most likely the stony indifference accorded to the unread. If it is a paper in a journal, it will not be reviewed at all. The publication remains on the record, and the academic receives credit for it; that is the way his trade works. But if the director commits a solecism of taste and judgement he fails in the most public of arenas. The reviewers deride him, and the audience shrivels. His future takes on the familiar insecurity of the theatre. If he succeeds in implementing a fresh perception, the rewards to his standing are instantaneous. There is in the theatre none of that time-lag between execution and reaction that insulates the academic against the immediate consequences of his work.

The theatre's investment in change is very great. Again, this used not to be true. Stanley Wells relates the story of an older actor, writing his acceptance of an invitation to play Kent in a provincial theatre, and adding: 'Usual moves, I suppose?'[9] Few anecdotes define more sharply the difference between the not-so-distant past and today. One still meets actors who will relate how Wolfit blocked out his roles, changing them in no way over many years. The business of Malvolio's letter scene, or with Pyramus and Thisbe, used to be hallowed. But the philosophy of 'Usual moves, I suppose?' is now anathema: every play, on the serious stage, is approached as though it were a new text.[10] Hence the paradox that the stage, that most traditional of institutions, is nowadays determined to prohibit a 'traditional' way of playing a classic. A whole landscape has been bulldozed away, as any moderately experienced playgoer can testify. Nothing like this proceeds in academe, where a decent respect for the past – much of it, after all, is still around – is usual. There are few directors of reputation today who were so twenty years ago; there are numerous critics. For all the reciprocity of stage-academic relations, the human cycles in each field are not synchronic.

These are background considerations, and they go some way towards supporting a premise of this book: that in the last half-generation the revaluation of Shakespeare has been led by the stage. The most interesting and influential reappraisals of certain plays have been launched by performances – and this in spite of the evidence one could accumulate that a given production owed something to an argument published in the scholarly press. Scholars differ; the stage concentrates, dramatizes, makes concrete and public. That was always true, but of late years certain changes in organization and leadership of the stage have enabled it to assume a larger share of the public regard. The stage has capitalized on its natural advantages.

The most striking feature of postwar theatre organization in England is the growth and dominance of the two great State companies, the National Theatre and the Royal Shakespeare Company. They now have exceptional standing in the English theatre. But they do not bear equally upon Shakespeare. The National Theatre, in spite of opening with O'Toole's Hamlet and providing in Olivier's Othello the most famous performance of the decade, has presented very little Shakespeare. It has preferred to leave him to the RSC, which for practical purposes is now the arbiter of Shakespeare on the English stage.

The RSC's title derived from 1961, shortly after Peter Hall became Director. 'It was generally felt that "Memorial" Theatre was not sufficiently expressive of the new, forward-looking company image that Hall wished to project, and was not in keeping with the role in which he wished to see the new RSC.'[11] The system that operated in the 1950s and earlier was based on a company that was reassembled each season. There was no question that this system repeatedly led to productions of the highest quality: one need only cite Brook's *Measure for Measure* (1950) and *Titus Andronicus* (1955), Gielgud's *Much Ado about Nothing* (1950) and *Twelfth Night* (1955), the Byam Shaw–Olivier *Macbeth* (1955), and Hall's *Twelfth Night* (1958). A new system, based on a settled company and greater emphasis on ensemble, was inaugurated under Peter Hall. Much of the new style of playing Shakespeare can be traced to a single technical innovation: the granting of three-year contracts to a number of artists. From this, much followed. An actor might work his way up from spear-carrying, through Rosencrantz–Salerio-type parts, to major roles. He would be involved in a continuity of discussion of Company style and methods; candour and openness of discussion were acknowledged features of the RSC ethos. (Directors were obliged to listen to their colleagues' criticisms at rehearsals.) The RSC's insistence upon a democratic ideal of ensemble playing, and its strong sense of community, harmonized with the continuity and security provided by the three-year contact.

The new system stressed studio work and, indeed, a continuing process of learning. Mime, fencing, movement were given much attention, through studio classes for which attendance was obligatory. Above all, verse-speaking was prominent in the Stratford drive to create a new style. 'I believe that theatre begins with the word' was Hall's credo.[12] 'The approach was analytical, straightforward and intelligent, and the resulting acting style was one of speaking the verse clearly with full respect to *meaning* and of stripping out all overlay of "word-music"; of "singing" or "declamatory" delivery. . .'[13] Hence, Robert Speaight's verdict on '. . . the Stratford style. My first impression is that every moment of every play is squeezed for the last ounce of meaning it contains.'[14] Intelligence in pursuit of meaning: that is the underlying plot of the RSC since Hall's directorate.

To that formula can be added John Elsom's characterization of the Company style: 'liveliness, social relevance, textual care and theatrical totality'.[15] The text deserves some elaboration. 'Liveliness' I need not linger over. Shakespeare has never been in danger of reverting to memorial-sculpture status at Stratford, and Elsom himself explains the quality as 'freshness of response'.[16] 'Social relevance' should be taken in conjunction with Peter Hall's repeated prescription that the Company should treat each play as though it had newly arrived in the morning's mail. While there was no question of the theatre promulgating an ideology, it was generally understood that the beliefs and ideals of the RSC were left of centre. On the whole, this was most evident in the Company's treatment of the histories. The hard sceptical scrutiny of power launched in *The Wars of the Roses* (1963) owed much to Brecht in its 'demythologizing' of authority. As Elsom notes,[17] the RSC concern for textual accuracy and scholarship acted as a check on the search for social relevance. In this respect, the appointment of John Barton (previously a Fellow of King's College, Cambridge) was of special importance. The RSC's respect for the text has been a strong element in its achievement, and I have documented numerous instances where the playing-text has shown only the lightest and most sensitive of cutting. It must, however, be added that the RSC, under Trevor Nunn, has adopted a more relaxed attitude to textual integrity. Cuts of some magnitude are now more commonplace than they used to be. The wholesale re-writing of *The Wars of the Roses* was extended in Barton's *King John* (1974), a much-criticized feat of director's licence. Textual fundamentalism was a stronger movement in the early 1960s than it is today. Still, it remains part of the RSC tradition – as are departures from it.

'Theatrical totality' takes us towards stage design. The most influential figure here is John Bury, who worked in close association with Hall during the 1960s. The accepted design-style in the 1950s was 'romantic realism', and the representative designer was Lila de Nobili. Her designs were painterly, with a strong suggestion of 'Old Master'. The 1960s saw a move away from decoration and elaboration towards a greater simplicity and selectivity. John Bury's work emphasized the textural image:

'I literally create in terms of scenery, floors, roofs, backwalls . . . one will get one's initial inspiration from the textural image often. One can take a bit of stone in one's hand and say – this is *Hamlet* . . . It isn't until I begin to create the model in terms of bits of stuff that I begin to think at all.' For *The Wars of the Roses*, *Hamlet* and other major productions of the sixties, Bury worked in terms of textured materials and substances which evolved from the initial design image. *The Wars of the Roses* had a steel image – and the settings and costumes were all created or textured in these terms. The black, glossy formica settings for *Hamlet* were an image of the enclosed, cold, political world of Elsinore as Peter Hall saw it.[18]

Simplicity became austerity in the next decade, with Christopher Morley the successor to John Bury. The 'white box' of Stratford, 1972, is possibly a terminus of design.[19] The strategy places a greater responsibility upon the actors. *Meaning* is created by actors acting. There is little else.

The final RSC innovation that demands mention here is the establishment of a London base at the Aldwych Theatre. Its purpose was to permit the Company to offer productions of contemporary plays. Thus, in the rhythm of RSC operations, Shakespeare is linked with the work of living dramatists. It often happens that a major hit at Stratford is transferred to London in the following season, where it goes into repertory with non-Shakespearean plays. The Company, then, has been largely successful in its ambition to detach Shakespeare from 'classic', 'summer-festival' status, and to install him as the leading playwright in a continuing series of diverse theatrical operations.[20] The ethos, the techniques and the sheer institutional magnitude of the RSC filter the Shakespeare we perceive on today's stage.

If organization, effectively, has become the RSC, leadership is the director. Though not of course confined to the RSC, directorial prominence is associated with it – most strikingly with Peter Brook. (He joined the RSC Directorate in 1962.) The rise of the director has been the great story of postwar theatre. It has been subject to continuing challenge, ranging from the routine apoplexies of those seeing a favourite play transformed to John Russell Brown's discriminating and penetrating critique in *Free Shakespeare*.[21] It does not seem necessary here to rehearse at length an elderly controversy. A single intelligence must select the text to be performed, analyse it, cast it, and arrange for its expressive presentation. These functions cannot be delegated, or settled in committee. The director must then bring that text into a living relation with today's audience, and recreate its vitality.

The aim is common to all directors of the first rank; and in practice they subscribe to it, however different their statements of policy might seem. Thus, Robin Phillips has said:

> The essential thing, by talking to the designer and the actors before you start, is to try and discover what the overall intention of the author is and you must try and find out that intention because from it spreads the feeling of whether the play is attacking or embracing you.[22]

Jonathan Miller has this:

> I don't believe one has any duty or obligation to an author, once he's dead. I think the concept of the public domain is very important in art, and that when a work in the performing arts has been finished, after the first, second or third try, during which I think one owes it to the author to honour his explicit conscious intention, and to co-operate with him and try and imagine it as it was when he wrote it, then after that it enters this curious zone of the public area and his aesthetic rights in it lapse. The play becomes a public object and one should be able to do to it exactly what one wants. The only rules to apply are those of aesthetic consistency, formal elegance and accuracy and artistic finesse, and need have no bearing on what the author actually meant.[23]

From these pronouncements one might conclude that Phillips and Miller are on opposite sides of an ideological fissure. On the contrary, each has directed Shakespeare in a way much praised for sensitivity and fidelity to the text. (The reader may like to compare their handling of *Measure for Measure*, in Chapter 2). In asserting their right to interpret the text – and, with it, contemporary society – in a mode that is freed from traditional prescriptions, directors acknowledge their kinship to each other, and perhaps their common debt to Peter Brook.[24]

Criticisms of the director, in his postwar apotheosis, tend to fall under two heads. One is that the freedom of the actors is diminished, that they have to fit into a predetermined pattern. Hence John Russell Brown's recommendation that the play be returned to the actors. It is not clear how this could be effected in terms of organization, nor that the result would not be the emergence of a deutero-director disguised, interestingly, as an actor. The second line of criticism aims at the productions, and alleges distortion of 'true' or 'straight' Shakespeare, through their reliance on stunts, and so on. To this, the directors reply that 'straight' Shakespeare does not exist, that it is merely a rhetorical synonym for a traditional manner of playing Shakespeare to which critics are attached. Peter Brook has elaborated upon the responsibility of a director:

A director picks up these texts and at once he is responsible. Anything he
does becomes a commitment. He cannot avoid this. An actor reads the lines
out loud. How? At once a thousand choices are before him. Does he read
tonelessly? Does he give the sense with no 'expressive' colour? Does he use
the intonations of realistic speech? Does he use a special voice? Does he
move towards song? . . . An actor who speaks must also be seen. How will
he appear? How will he be dressed? . . . None of these questions can be
ducked.[25]

In itself, this passage disposes of the 'straight' Shakespeare argument.
A more searching variant of the second criticism is that a director may
well seize on a thematic idea that is genuinely present in the text and
concentrate on it to the exclusion of the others. Here critics tend to
underrate the enormous richness of ideational content in a Shakespeare
play, and the need for a director to focus a production so that a
portion, at least, of that richness makes brilliant impact. Naturally,
directors often make public claims (*'King Lear* is about the failure of
authority on two levels')[26] that appear as overbids and invite retri-
bution. But the need to provide a metaphoric vehicle, and with it an
intellectual 'fix' on the play, is an essential function of the director.
Ultimately, the criticisms come down to the difference between the
first-rate and the rest. Directors of the first rank bear their justifications with them; the others do not. In any event, it is hard to
disagree with Peter Hall's view of the matter:

If I walk into the Louvre and paint a large black moustache on the face of
the Mona Lisa, it's there for ever, defaced. But if I do *Macbeth* – as I did –
in red rugs, I make nobody a fool but myself. *Macbeth* is still there at the
end – staring at me. I have done nothing to *Macbeth*.[27]

The text remains: the productions supplement each other and are, if
good, compatible with the text. It is impossible to conceive of a
production that represents a Shakespeare play on a one-to-one
correspondence.

Let *Measure for Measure* focus the argument. It is usual to regard the
ending of *Measure for Measure* as a spectacular instance of the lack of
collateral instructions Shakespeare gives for performance. One can
reverse this way of looking at it. It is possible to regard the entire text
as a single extended stage direction which governs a single action:
Isabella's response to the Duke's proposal. In determining this action
the director determines the provisional meaning of the play.
     This act of determination is of necessity unambiguous. The play
moves out of the realm of psychic shadows, and permits a light to fall

on the motives of the central figures. The Duke, who has disclaimed the smallest interest in women, proposes marriage; Isabella, the novitiate nun, must react. The actress may convey a willing or terrified acceptance, or a rejection, or she may remain undecided; but even a state of indecision contains an inflection, and therefore a judgement, not to be evaded. Several major possibilities exist, but they are mutually exclusive. The alternative view is registered in Kenneth Muir's prescription: 'Any good production of *Measure for Measure* would necessarily present us with the possibility that Duke Vincentio was a symbol of divine providence, or an earthly ruler who was God's steward, or a puppet-master, or a busybody. It is not the business of the director to choose one of these and exclude the others.'[28] One pronounces with diffidence on what it is the business of other professionals to do; but I surmise that directors, who have their living to make, reckon that it is bound up with decisive choice of interpretation. What looks like ambiguity to the priesthood might, to a lay audience, seem plain confusion. I find it hard to conceive of an Isabella simultaneously exercising her options of prostrating herself before divine Providence, accepting joyfully the hand of an earthly ruler, registering womanly indignation at the unmasking of a puppet-master, and sending a busybody about his business.

I turn from the metaphysical athletics of the ideal production to the ones we actually get. In the past decade they have swung decisively against the model-prince–providential-ruler view of *Measure for Measure*. A director will not, usually, close out all his options with the hard severity of a Brecht demonstration, but the line of his strategic advance will be clear to the audience. With *Measure for Measure*, the actions of the central figure are today construed in a manner radically altered from the past. Our mental model of the play has changed, and the stage demonstrates the new fact. Moreover, it is impossible to believe that the revaluation of *Measure for Measure* is attributable to a vagrant shift in fashion (scholarly or theatrical), a random oscillation in received values. Scholarship, which is well aware of the schizoid nature of *Measure for Measure* (the metaphor is Tillyard's) has not changed its readings substantially over the past generation. What has changed is the general audience. It is not, as I take it, receptive to the proposition that Authority Knows Best; and half of it consists of women, who tend now to a certain scepticism at the idea that Isabella will *of course* accept the Duke's hand. We are talking of a shift in the general perception. The changes in the staging of *Measure for Measure* relate, at bottom, to a changed directorial sense of what the audience can perceive, and tolerate in its action.

What is true for *Measure for Measure* is equally, though less spectacularly, true for other plays in the canon. The choice of plays in this book reflects primarily my sense of the most interesting shifts in staging, allied to the general perception. I hesitated over including *King Lear*, but eventually concluded that the dominant fact was a single revolutionary production which has been well documented.[29] The Brook–Scofield *Lear* for the RSC (1962), later made into a film, is the most celebrated version of our times. Kenneth Tynan's review says most of what needs saying here:

> Lay him to rest, the royal Lear with whom generations of star actors have made us reverently familiar; the majestic ancient, wronged and maddened by his vicious daughters; the felled giant, beside whose bulk the other characters crouch like pygmies. Lay also to rest the archaic notion that Lear is automatically entitled to our sympathy because he is a king who suffers.
>
> A great director (Peter Brook) has scanned the text with fresh eyes and discovered a new protagonist – not the booming, righteously indignant Titan of old, but an edgy, capricious old man, intensely difficult to live with. In short, he has dared to direct *King Lear* from a standpoint of moral neutrality.[30]

Grigori Kozintsev's film *King Lear*, movingly distilled into his book *King Lear: The Space of Tragedy* (1977), has not yet had the circulation and impact that would warrant extended discussion here. It offers some conceptual parallels to Brook's version. Kozintsev re-examines the 'heroic' quality of Lear: 'is he a heroic personality from the beginning? No, Lear is rather the tragedy of a personality who flattered himself into thinking he was heroic. He becomes great only when he understands that he is like any other man.'[31] In keeping with this approach, this Lear, Yuri Yarvet, was small, slender. An Esthonian, he did not even speak Russian well. But 'I looked at Yarvet and recognized Lear'.[32] The nadir of Lear's sufferings on the heath becomes, for Kozintsev, the night in the hovel.

> The essence is not the pigs but the night spent outside the boundaries of life – that is what is important; the very lowest rung of nature, a spark of animal warmth, almost dying in the icy darkness of the universe. As far as I see it, it is here that the highest point, the climax of the storm takes place; the climax is in the dirty bodies, lying about in the rotten straw, not in the flashing of studio lightning and the deluge produced by the firemen's technical expertise.[33]

This – Kozintsev makes the comparison with Dostoevsky's penal settlement wash-house – constitutes Lear's purgatory before he is redeemed to humanity.

There is no close identity between Brook and Kozintsev, certainly. Brook's production was 'amoral because it is set in an amoral universe. For him the play is a mighty philosophic farce in which the leading figures enact their roles on a gradually denuded stage that resembles, at the end, a deserted graveyard or unpeopled planet.'[34] It owed much to Jan Kott's discussion, which linked *King Lear* with Samuel Beckett's *Endgame*.[35] Kozintsev saw Lear as an emotionless despot, who rediscovers his humanity through suffering. But both question the 'Titan' stereotype. There is no 'modern' reading of *King Lear*, other than a determination to bring its protagonist within the fold of common humanity.[36]

The plays studied here have, for me, largely chosen themselves. The abrupt changes in our sense of *Measure for Measure* and *Henry V* demand their inclusion. *Coriolanus*, in its long traverse from Right to Left, and then away to something not strictly political at all, still seems the major test of the 'political' element in Shakespeare. That great *Rohrschach*, *Hamlet*, accommodates itself effortlessly to all eras. It is here for much the same reasons as it figures in so many repertory seasons. Similarly, *Twelfth Night* is the most often performed of all Shakespeare's comedies. It seems now a dark comedy, an associate of *All's Well That Ends Well* and *Measure for Measure*. *Troilus and Cressida* has no known stage history prior to 1898, and has only come to be performed regularly in the past generation. 'For the stage director,' as Bernard Beckerman observes, '*Troilus and Cressida* is virtually a new work.'[37] Something of a cult among directors, *Troilus and Cressida* has strong claims to be *the* Shakespeare for our time. All six plays here are seen regularly nowadays. They may be thought of as belonging to the inner repertory of the Shakespeare canon.

My approach to the six plays is rigorously eclectic, consistently unsystematic. Each play has its own qualities, and presents special problems, to which one must adjust. The plays operate on a different time-scale of perception, for one thing. *Coriolanus* has moved slowly across a considerable expanse of social time. *Henry V* changed decisively in the 1960s, visibly in the RSC production of 1964. The staging of *Measure for Measure* has been well documented to 1970, precisely the point at which its changes become most interesting. Then again, the number of productions to consider, or select from, varies greatly. There are many more productions of *Twelfth Night* to choose from than of *Troilus and Cressida*. What is the principle of selection? It can only be significance. And this applies not only to the intrinsic quality of the production, but also to its national frame. It is a matter of judgement, and there is no formula to which one can hand over one's judgement. If one hardens on to the English stage category, productions of interest and value elsewhere are excluded. And this would be a pity, especially in view of the international quality of the stage and the extent to which the major theatrical centres are aware of what the others are doing. If one widens the formal scope, an enormous mass of data has to be processed, most of it national and provincial in interest. It seems best to concentrate on the English stage, and make, on occasion, an intelligent cast outside. It would be absurd to exclude the 'Stavisky' *Coriolanus*, the major achievements of the Canadian and American Stratfords, Olivier's film of *Henry V*, or Daly's (in essence) Anglo-American productions, on a formula. Nevertheless, the French, Canadian and American stages lie outside my main field of inquiry, as does the film. My focus at all times is on *the play*, and the way in which the play has been interpreted on stage.

I should add that I have seen many of the productions described in this book, beginning with Scofield's *Hamlet* at Stratford-upon-Avon in 1948. But I am not in this instance a reviewer, nor can I formally indicate a different status for the productions I have not seen. The basis of this book must be public documentation. So I have preferred not to identify those productions which I encountered at first hand. Still, the sense of performance values which they have imparted is, I hope, assimilated into this book.

The studies presented here concentrate on the idea of each production, as revealed through a variety of sources: directors' pronouncements, programme-notes, the playing-text, the known characteristics of the leading actors, the reviews. I take my evidence where I can get it. The discussion of each play, and each production, is necessarily partial and selective. For instance, Hector is a fairly substantial acting-part, but I have virtually ignored him in my treatment of *Troilus and Cressida:* Thersites and Ulysses, especially, offer a much better guide to the director's intention and the impact of the production. The effect of casting is varyingly important. One cannot discuss *Hamlet* without a full awareness of the values physicalized in the leading actor. With *Troilus and Cressida* there is really little to say, for the title roles have merely to be filled by attractive young people, that is all. The twin staples of these studies are the prompt-books and the reviews. Concerning prompt-books, I have come to appreciate the force of Charles H. Shattuck's warning:

Promptbooks are tricky, secretive, stubborn informants. They chatter and exclaim about what we hardly need to know: that certain characters are being readied by the callboy to make their entrances; that the scene is about to change or the curtain to drop; that the orchestra is about to play at the act-end. They fall blackly silent just when we most hope to be told where the actor stood or how he looked or what he did. Rarely do they give us a hint of voice or temper or histrionic manner. They tell lies, as anybody knows who ever produced a play and failed to write into the book his own last-minute revisions or the happy inspirations that come to the actors midway in a run of performances.[38]

I give a single instance of the problems, from my researches. On the discovery scene in *Troilus and Cressida*, a reviewer of unquestioned excellence wrote, in a passage criticizing Troilus' acting, '. . . and the great speech – "this is, and is not, Cressid" – which should sound the motto of the play, went for nothing'. But the prompt-text reveals a cut from 'Bifold authority' to 'As Ariachne's broken woof to enter'. Troilus could hardly be expected to make anything of a line not in his part. Do we, then, conclude that a distinguished critic nodded? I think not: the director may have reinstated the cut passage. Or Troilus may have forgotten that he was supposed to omit it. Or perhaps he experimented one night. That Troilus is now dead, and cannot be consulted. The prompt-book remains – and it is, after all, a sure guide to the director's strategic intentions. With *Hamlet* and *Troilus and Cressida* especially, I have considered the cuts with some care, since they offer vital clues – which are not, usually, picked up by reviewers. Theatre critics record impressions and effects, prompt-texts express intentions. Between them they offer the surest means of tracing that most transient of identities, the visible shape of Shakespeare as he moves across the stage.

NOTES

1 A detailed study of the changes in stage presentation is available in Dennis Bartholomeusz, *Macbeth and the Players* (Cambridge: Cambridge University Press, 1969); and in Marvin Rosenberg, *The Masks of Macbeth* (Berkeley, Calif: University of California Press, 1978).

2 Something of this emerges in J. C. Trewin's survey of productions, *Shakespeare on the English Stage 1900–1964* (London: Barrie and Rockliff, 1964). J. L. Styan, in *The Shakespeare Revolution: Criticism and Performance in the Twentieth Century* (Cambridge: Cambridge University Press, 1977), offers a more penetrating analysis. The dual theme here is the evolution of superior methods in the theatre, and the *rapprochement* between theatre and scholarship.

3 Shakespeare's technique of interweaving contrary impressions is acutely analysed by E. A. J. Honigmann in *Shakespeare: Seven Tragedies: The Dramatist's Manipulation of Response* (London: Macmillan, 1976).

4   Bernard Levin, *The Pendulum Years* (London: Jonathan Cape, 1970); Christopher Booker, *The Neophiliacs: A Study of the Revolution in the Fifties and Sixties* (London: Collins, 1969).
5   Booker, op. cit., p. 35.
6   John Elsom, *Postwar British Theatre* (London: Routledge & Kegan Paul, 1976), p. 75.
7   Sheridan Morley, 'Rattigan at 65', *The Times*, 9 May 1977.
8   Stanley Wells, 'The academic and the theatre', in *The Triple Bond: Plays, Mainly Shakespearean, in Performance*, ed. Joseph G. Price (University Park, Pa., and London: University of Pennsylvania Press, 1975), p. 3.
9   Wells, op. cit., p. 9.
10 Even so, a more cautious view of this tendency is expressed by A.C. Sprague and J. C. Trewin in *Shakespeare's Plays Today: Customs and Conventions of the Stage* (Columbia, University of South Carolina Press, 1971), p. 20. The underlying truths that tradition has established may still influence a production.
11 David Addenbrooke, *The Royal Shakespeare Company* (London: William Kimber, 1974), p. 48. In this section I have drawn extensively upon Addenbrooke's authoritative account of the RSC during the Peter Hall years.
12 Ibid., p. 89.
13 Ibid., p. 90.
14 Robert Speaight, 'Shakespeare in Britain', *Shakespeare Quarterly*, vol. XV (1964), p. 388.
15 Elsom, op. cit., p. 170.
16 Ibid., p. 170.
17 Ibid., p. 171.
18 Addenbrooke, op. cit., p. 110.
19 An extended account of RSC design evolution will be found in John Russell Brown, *Free Shakespeare* (London: Heinemann, 1974), pp. 19–28.
20 Addenbrooke (op. cit., pp. 272–82) gives as appendix 5 a complete list of RSC stage productions 1960–71.
21 Among the best-informed critiques of the directors, see also Bernard Beckerman, 'The flowers of fancy, the jerks of invention, or, directorial approaches to Shakespeare', in *Shakespeare 1971: Proceedings of the World Shakespeare Congress, Vancouver, August 1971*, ed. Clifford Leech and J. M. R. Margeson (Toronto: University of Toronto Press, 1972), pp. 200–14.
22 Judith Cook, *Directors' Theatre* (London: Harrap, 1974), p. 126.
23 Ibid., p. 101.
24 For a recent statement by Peter Brook concerning his methods of directing Shakespeare, see my *On Directing Shakespeare: Interviews with Contemporary Directors* (London and New York: Croom Helm and Barnes & Noble, 1977), pp. 113–30.
25 Peter Brook, 'Production: total responsibility of a director', *The Birmingham Post*, 17 April 1964. Quoted in Brown, op. cit., pp. 9–10.
26 Jonathan Miller, quoted in Brown, op. cit., p. 12.
27 Addenbrooke, op. cit., p. 98.
28 Kenneth Muir, 'The critic, the director, and liberty of interpreting', in *The Triple Bond*, ed. Price, p. 28.
29 For example, by Charles Marowitz, in 'Lear log', *Encore*, vol. 10, January/February 1963; by Styan, op. cit., 217–23; and by Peter Brook. See especially Brook's *The Empty Space* (Harmondsworth: Penguin, 1972), pp. 16–17, 25–6, 102–6.

30 This review is printed in Kenneth Tynan, *A View of the English Stage* (Frogmore, St Albans: Paladin, 1976), p. 343.

31 Grigori Kozintsev, *King Lear: The Space of Tragedy* (London: Heinemann, 1977), p. 62.

32 Ibid., p. 76.

33 Ibid., p. 192.

34 Tynan, op. cit., p. 346.

35 Jan Kott, *Shakespeare Our Contemporary*, 2nd edn. (London: Methuen, 1967).

36 The same tendency is visible in Peter Ustinov's remarkable Lear, directed by Robin Phillips, at Stratford, Ontario (1979-80). Ustinov presented a study of extreme old age, observed with as much humanity as precision. See my review in 'Stratford Festival Canada', *Shakespeare Quarterly*, vol. XXXI (1980), pp. 174–5.

37 *The Festival Shakespeare 'Troilus and Cressida'*, ed. Bernard Beckerman and Joseph Papp (New York: Macmillan, 1967), p. 20.

38 Charles H. Shattuck, *The Shakespeare Promptbooks: A Descriptive Catalogue* (Urbana, Ill., and London: University of Illinois Press, 1965), p. 3.

CHAPTER ONE

The Metamorphoses of *Coriolanus*

The search for meanings in Shakespeare leads to one kind of outward manifestation, the stage production; and the history of these productions is a sampling, or refraction, of the cultural history of their times.[1] This is obvious enough, and applies to all of Shakespeare's plays. But *Coriolanus* is a special case. It is, by general consent, 'the most exclusively political play by Shakespeare'.[2] The play depicts an especially bitter class-struggle, and focuses on the failings of a singularly unlikeable aristocrat; it therefore stimulates, to a greater degree than any other play in the canon, the political feelings and attitudes of a normal audience. Nevertheless, the general thrust of the play has never been decisively demonstrated.

> Careful critics and casual audiences alike, feeling the immediate impact of the play, have, according to their considered opinions or momentary prejudice, variously regarded it as an impartial presentation of the secular struggle between the few and the many, a whole-hearted indictment of democracy, or an ardent profession of faith in the aristocratic principle.[3]

The text offers much sustenance to Left and to Right; so much is clear. The play depends, for its continued vitality and provisional meaning, very considerably upon the circumstances of a given production, and it is this aspect of the matter that concerns us here. I do not propose here a full stage history of *Coriolanus*, but I shall consider some of the most important stage versions of the play and show how their handling of the political issues – and the character of the hero – is a touchstone to the life of the times.

I

The seventeenth- and eighteenth-century acting-versions of *Coriolanus* have, as we should expect, a mild curiosity value. Little need be said of Nahum Tate's *The Ingratitude of a Commonwealth, or The Fall of Coriolanus* (1682). It is a butchery of Shakespeare on a par with his happy ending to *King Lear*. Still, a political idea of a sort is struggling to be set free. The tendentious title makes its own point; and the Dedicatory Epistle points out 'a Resemblance' to 'the busie Faction of our own times'. The play's 'Moral' then becomes 'to Recommend Submission and Adherence to Establisht Lawful Power'.[4] Crude as this is, it is probably true that all the later interpretations of *Coriolanus* have to take a stand on whether Tate's moral is essentially sound. A superficial political relevance attaches itself to John Dennis' version, *The Invader of His Country, or The Fatal Resentment* (1719). But this is mere opportunism; Dennis is writing in the wake of the Jacobite rebellion of 1715, and playing up an obvious analogy of situation.[5] There is no real attempt at understanding and expounding Shakespeare here. As for the mid-century versions, James Thomson's *Coriolanus* is less an adaptation than a new play, and Thomas Sheridan's *Coriolanus, or The Roman Matron* (1752) is a mélange of Thomson and Shakespeare. It is not until John Philip Kemble's production (first staged in 1789) that we encounter a version of *Coriolanus* that demands to be taken seriously as a capable, sustained and celebrated attempt to expound the play to a contemporary audience.

II

Kemble was the Coriolanus of his day. The part was his, from 1789 to 1817; he chose it for his farewell performance in that year, and the testimonial dinner that followed was explicitly dedicated to the 'Hero of Corioli'. The text that Kemble played was a cut version of Shakespeare, for three Acts.[6] Thereafter an infusion of Thomson was introduced. The main effect was to strengthen the jealousy motive of Aufidius, thus giving the gallery a situation it could more readily appreciate. Notwithstanding some Thomsonian sentimentalism in Act V, the text is very far from a travesty of Shakespeare. What of the production? It aspired, first, to historical accuracy. The attempt at reproducing Roman costume, architecture and so on was widely acclaimed, but one may question the underlying fidelity of such an approach. The historically accurate is a species of literalism; it serves the purposes of the spectacular; the spectacular is, simply, a harmless mode of entertainment. *The Times* takes its eulogy to the point of incongruity: 'The ceremony of the ovation on *Caius Marcius's* triumphant return from *Corioli* is superb; and we think the pains and cost bestowed upon it, much better bestowed than on the ballets we have seen, or those which, we hear, are forthcoming.'[7]

Kemble's performance appears to have been a study in marble pride. On this, the critics agree. Leigh Hunt has this:

> . . . the same faults of style that prevent him from being a great general tragedian, particularly in characters of sensibility and variety, are of assistance to him in certain parts of loftiness and austerity which he has almost exclusively made his own. Of this description are *Coriolanus*, and the misanthropic character of *Penruddock* in the *Wheel of Fortune*. The haughtiness and rigidity which are only disagreeable intrusions upon most of his tragic parts here come in aid of the actual characters to be represented. . . .'[8]

And Hazlitt:

> The range of characters, in which Mr Kemble shines, and is superior to every other actor, are those which consist in the development of some one sentiment or exclusive passion. . . . So in Coriolanus, he exhibits the ruling passion with the same continued firmness, he preserves the same haughty dignity of demeanour, the same energy of will, and unbending sternness of temper throughout.[9]

The role, then, is projected as a single intense humour – that of rigid pride. And this is the aspect that the contemporary illustrations reveal. When one sifts through the illustrations of Kemble as Coriolanus in the Enthoven Collection, one finds always the same image emerging. It is of Kemble – looking stern, forbidding and dyspeptic – striking the appropriate posture for 'No; I'll die here . . .'. That such a line should be chosen to typify the hero tells us much about the concept of the part. I submit that the presentation of Coriolanus as a statue in marble, set in the context of a historical pageant, tends to divert attention from the political issues of the play.

And yet the issues refuse to be dissipated. Hazlitt writes trenchantly of them, following a Kemble performance in December 1816. He inclines to regard the play as being written from the right-wing point of view: 'Shakespeare himself seems to have had a leaning to the arbitrary side of the question, perhaps from some feeling of contempt for his own origin; and to have spared no occasion of baiting the rabble.'[10] Nevertheless, Hazlitt's analysis of Coriolanus' actions is devastating.

> Coriolanus complains of the fickleness of the people: yet the instant he cannot gratify his pride and obstinacy at their expense, he turns his arms against his country. If his country was not worth defending, why did he build his pride on its defence? He is a conqueror and a hero; he conquers

other countries, and makes this a plea for enslaving his own; and when he is prevented from doing so, he leagues with its enemies to destroy his country. He rates the people 'as if he were a God to punish, and not a man of their infirmity'. He scoffs at one of their tribunes for maintaining their rites and franchises: 'Mark you his absolute *shall?*' not marking his own absolute *will* to take everything from them; his impatience of the slightest opposition to his own pretensions being in proportion to their arrogance and absurdity.[11]

And his conclusion is: 'The whole dramatic moral of *Coriolanus* is, that those who have little shall have less, and that those who have much shall take all that others have left.'[12] It will be seen that Hazlitt has a secure grasp of the play. While not minimizing Shakespeare's unillusioned treatment of the Roman crowd, he recognizes that the patrician claims are refuted. His mordant analysis of Coriolanus' failings closes the easy exit from the play's problems – the view that Coriolanus is 'only' a man of intense pride. (Such a view is not incompatible with a certain sympathy for the man.) One has to respect Kemble's giant and sustained attempts to bring back Shakespeare to the English stage on the proper terms. But Hazlitt's criticism is of a higher order, perhaps, than Kemble's *Coriolanus* merited.

III

Kean, as I guess, reached much farther towards the heart of the role. His performance of Coriolanus in January 1820 was accounted a failure, and played for four nights only. But this was because the accepted style of playing the part was firmly established as Kemble's. We learn, for instance, that Kean's small figure was unsuitable for the hero. But why should not Coriolanus be small? The text gives ample foundation. The images of acting, with their suggestion of striving for identity, make a point that is very clear in Volumnia's charge: 'You might have been enough the man you are/With striving less to be so' (III, ii, 19–20). And Coriolanus' maddened reiteration of 'boy' in the final scene – it is Aufidius' supreme insult, as he well knows – makes additionally good sense if, in fact, Coriolanus is small, even boyish, in stature. Now, Kemble's concept entailed the appearance, and the reality, of *size*. Again, Hazlitt remarks that Kean did not communicate a sublime contempt for the people: his 'I banish you', we are told, 'was given with all the virulence of execration and rage of impotent despair'.[13] Well, and why not? A modern actor is surely compelled to regard '*I* banish *you*' as a childishness, an attempt to deny reality through an effusion of will. A contemporary playgoer makes the distinction nicely here: he contrasts Phelps' 'sublimity of disdain' with Kean's cry of 'ungovernable passion'.[14] Granted that the sublime is not a mode that appeals to the twentieth century, I suspect that Kean's interpretation of the role was far closer to what we have come to regard as its truth. His genius was ahead of his time, and he could not communicate the truth of the play to his audience.[15]

IV

Macready's Coriolanus was not a great one, though he appeared in it with some success[16] in five seasons between 1819 and 1839. Leigh Hunt's reservations seem convincing: 'But we doubt whether Mr Macready's graceful gestures and shapely movements are not somewhat too elegant for *Coriolanus*; perhaps we should say, too softly elegant and swimming.'[17] The part was evidently played against the grain of the text for a certain style and effect. But I wish to single out an excellence, and a most significant one, in the celebrated 1838 production. This belonged to the historical–spectacular category; it employed a huge cast; the stage designs and costumes were sumptuous. Simply a more expansive and expensive repeat performance of Kemble's, we may think. But note this:

> When the stage becomes animated with a seemingly countless mob of barbarians, armed with staves, mattocks, hatchets, pickaxes, and their wrongs, we become sensible that it is not merely a coward crowd before us, but the onward and increasing wave . . . of men who have spied their way to equal franchises, and are determined to fight their way to the goal. There is no mistaking the struggle for power that has begun. It is not noble against serf, but against freeman. The illusion is still further maintained by their dress. They are no longer the mere *tunicatus popellus*, who have hitherto caricatured the Roman commonalty. In many there is an approximation to the toga; and the squalor . . . is altogether done away with . . . Rome is there rough-hewn, and her sons breathe her own rude majesty.[18]

One wonders: 1838 is not 1819, certainly. Six years after the passage of the Reform Bill is not the climate of Peterloo. It must have been possible to conceive, and communicate theatrically, the point that the men of Rome on their way to 'equal franchises' have their counterpart in the England of Victoria. The reviewer in *John Bull* (a Radical journal) evidently regards the historic process depicted in the production with equanimity, and his implied historical analogy is clear enough.

Generally, we have to remember that there are two areas of supreme importance in *Coriolanus*, through which a production must communicate the truth of the play: one is the character of Coriolanus, the other is the crowd. We can take it that all productions prior to the nineteenth century (and perhaps prior to Macready) presented the Roman crowd as a mob – repellent, filthy, fickle. Macready's achievement is to display a crowd that has ceased to be a mob and is in the process of becoming a segment of the people. It is a segment of some character and dignity; it has aspirations; and by readjusting the balance of dramatic sympathies it makes a profound case against Coriolanus.

V

I pass over two important Coriolanuses of the later nineteenth century, Forrest and Phelps. They appear to have been studies in marble grandeur and sublime pride, a mode sufficiently known to us from their predecessors. Instead, I select two Coriolanuses who happened to appear within two months of each other (and the death of Queen Victoria) in 1901: Benson and Irving.

Both productions followed highly compressed texts. The battle scenes before Corioli, for instance, were eliminated. *The Times* thought little of the play: 'the dramatic interest is too scrappy for the great public to delight in it'.[19] It reviewed favourably F. R. Benson's production, however. The crowd was especially commended: '. . . cleverly handled . . . worked a cold house up, first to warmth and then to enthusiasm . . . Absence of plot, absence of love story, scrappiness of situation – all was forgotten in the stirring conflict of factions, the sick hurry of popular passions, played upon by the divided aims of the patricians and the plebs.'[20] A crowd, then, of great vitality, and a political conflict presented with a certain impartiality. Moreover – and this is rare, if not new – the part of Sicinius Velutus is singled out for praise: 'Mr Oscar Asche's grimly humorous demagogue, whose counterpart might be found in Hyde Park any Sunday . . .'[21] R. Dickins found the part equally impressive:

> The Sicinius Velutus of Oscar Asche was in its way almost equally good – strong, coarse-minded, selfish and cunning, he represented to perfection the contemptible creature the author intended. I can still see him, after the expulsion of Coriolanus, seated on a stone in the Roman street, contentedly peeling and eating an orange.[22]

Dickins' own sentiments are transparent; but in the point is that the
importance of the popular tribunes was fully grasped in the production, and by the audience. As for Benson's Coriolanus, this
appears to have been rather lightweight. 'Mr Benson's Coriolanus is
an athletic, boyish Roman – rightly young, since Menenius speaks of
him as "son", and rightly, as we think, showing at first towards the
common folk rather a humorous contempt than a settled indignation.'[23] This strikes me as a compromise with the difficulties of the
part. On the one hand, the 'boyish' approach links up with the Kean
tradition. On the other, the 'humorous contempt' invites audience
sympathy, and plays down the rancour of the part. Imagine the
'humorous contempt' in

> What's the matter, you dissentious rogues,
> That, rubbing the poor itch of your opinion,
> Make yourselves scabs?

Dickins' judgement was that 'Benson was not big enough for Caius –
not big enough in personality, or power, or inches, and without a
convincing Caius we cannot have a successful Coriolanus.'[24]

It seems likely that Benson did not succeed in focusing or carrying
the play. Irving's Coriolanus of two months later was the last
Shakespearian performance of his career. We should expect it to
contain some central virtues, and the records bear this out. The
production was splendidly mounted – the scenery and costume
designs having been commissioned from Alma-Tadema: a sumptuous
setting for a major central performance. Once again, the crowd
receives special praise:

> And what a crowd it is! As everyone knows, the crowd is a protagonist in this
> play, and everything depends upon the power of the stage management to
> give it life, individuality, diversity. That power is certainly not lacking at the
> Lyceum. Whether the crowd is hooting or acclaiming Coriolanus, listening
> open-mouthed to its tribunes, or arguing fatuously with itself, we are made to
> feel that it is a genuine mob and no mere pack of 'supernumeraries'.[25]

Predictably, Irving's performance was in the heroic mould; none of
the Kean–Benson boyishness for him, no hint of flaws in the marble.
Symons saw him as 'a kind of Roman Moltke, the lean, thoughtful
soldier, he spoke throughout with a slow, contemptuous enunciation,
as of one only just not too lofty to sneer . . . And his pride was an
intellectual pride; the weakness of a character, but the angry dignity
of a temperament.'[26] *The Times*'s reviewer chose to compare Kemble's

method 'the sublime', with today's, 'the natural': but the object of the
reviewer's gaze seems rather a modernization of the sublime than an
antithesis to it. 'Coriolanus makes a splendid central figure – a rugged
soldier, all compact of heroic stuff, hating praise, despising weakness,
towering by sheer force and inflexibility of character above his
fellows.'[27]
The most interesting criticism comes, I think, from Dickins. He
does not care for Irving's performance, and he advances this justification for his opinion: 'For Caius to interest and move an audience
the part must surely be approached from the point of view of the
Patricians, and Irving appeared to view it from the standpoint of the
Plebeians.'[28] Here, I suggest is the key to the play's difficulties in
performance. To present Coriolanus with a degree of sympathy (and
this may be solicited in various ways) is, essentially, to take the
patricians' side, and the people's case is necessarily weakened thereby.
To adopt the popular standpoint is, naturally, to see a repellent and
threatening figure – a conception that may fail to appeal to the
distinguished actor who normally takes the role. There is logically a
third possibility, which Dickins does not mention: that both factions
are drawn with entire detachment. Irving's *Coriolanus* may have
belonged to this category. Even so, a production that disengages itself
from implicit support of the central figure is, insidiously, posing the
only question that really matters. Whose side is the play on?

VI

This essay is primarily concerned with English-language productions
of *Coriolanus;* still, by way of interlude, I cannot resist citing a *locus
classicus* in the French response to the question. The production
mounted at the Comédie Française on 9 December 1933 soon found
itself a part of the disturbance that led, in the wake of the Stavisky
scandals,[29] to the fall of the Daladier government in February 1934. It
seems that the play was received as a right-wing polemic, hence as an
attack on the Socialist Government of the day. As such, it was
enthusiastically applauded by the opponents of the Government, and
turned into a focal point of the rioting that intensified the political
crisis. Eventually the Government moved against those responsible for
the production, and *The Times* of 6 February 1934 carried a news
report of the supersession of M. Fabre, Director of the Comédie
Française. 'Moreover, the incident coincides with a very successful
production of *Coriolanus* which has been drawing crowded houses for

some time; and since *Coriolanus* is admittedly a damaging critique of popular institutions, Ministers did not escape the suspicion of having been moved by political spite against M. Fabre.' Both the text and the production are thus taken to be critical of the popular cause. *The Times'* editorial of the same day testifies to the impact of the production.

> Not content with applauding uproariously the contemptuous condemnation of mob-rule by Shakespeare's Coriolanus at the Comédie Française, the Camelots du Roi have been more responsible than any other factions for having turned the neighbourhood of the Chamber, the inner boulevards, and the Place de l'Opéra into impassable mobs of fighting citizens.

The difficulties of the Daladier government led shortly to its replacement by the administration of M. Doumergue, and on 20 February *The Times* printed an authoritative signed article by John Palmer on the significance of the *Coriolanus* affair: '. . . the admirable version of M. René-Louis Piachaud', he explained, 'was suspected of being a deliberately tendentious and topical version, intended to discredit Parliamentary institutions and to pave the way for a dictatorship in France'.[30] For this suspicion, apparently, there was no shred of evidence; M. Piachaud, a scholar-recluse, denied any such aim. But the public took it as an attack on corruption in high places, as well as on parliamentary institutions.

> The lines which elicited violent approval were those which derided public men. The farewell of Menenius to the Tribunes, *adieu mauvais bergers du troupeau populaire*, was a call to arms. Such sallies as the exclamation of Coriolanus: *Bon, vous vendez le consulat, alors. Combien?* were received with exclamations of delight . . . But for the tragic disorders which followed upon the Stavisky scandals *Coriolanus* would have run its course. The Paris disorders and the temporary suspension of party government which followed them converted, however, a general indictment into something of the nature of a political manifesto. The observations of Coriolanus were then applauded or denounced as an attack upon the whole system of party Government, and the Comédie Française became a public arena.[31]

One needs, then, to qualify the main feature of the 'Stavisky' *Coriolanus:* the fact that it served as a channel – better, a lightning-conductor – for anti-democratic passions. Text and production, whether deliberately pointed up or not, crystallized a specific situation in the France of the day. Such a fable, however relevant to the Paris of 1933–4, is in fact entirely atypical of modern *Coriolanus* productions. I know of no successor – if we exclude Osborne's *A Place Calling Itself Rome* – that openly takes the play to be an anti-democratic tract.

VII

In fact, *Coriolanus* producers of the postwar period have not been notably interested in the play as a political tract. No doubt this reflects the, on the whole, lowered social tensions of the past generation. Directors, in their symbiotic relationship with the public, have perceived that it will not do to make the audience's flesh creep with apocalyptic visions of the class-war fought *à l'outrance*. The political element in *Coriolanus* is very great, and can never be concealed; but it is not the exclusive concern of the play. Moreover, there is a certain obviousness about the political content of *Coriolanus* that scarcely appeals to a modern director, on his mettle to find a new and challenging vista on the play. Coriolanus as a symptom of social malfunctioning is more interesting than Coriolanus as the *donnée* in a prescribed political thesis. Consequently, the producers of late years have, as I judge, been consistently attracted to those elements in the play that fall outside the limits of politics, strictly defined. I illustrate my point with productions from the past thirty years.

Anthony Quayle's Coriolanus (directed by Glen Byam Shaw) at Stratford in 1952 seems to have been a good middle-of-the-road production. *The Times'* review gives us the key:

> Mr Anthony Quayle, taking the legitimate view that scorn of the mob need not imply a patrician temperament, presents the hero as a tough soldier with a parade-ground rasp in his voice, wearing his wounds aggressively as badges of rank. This is a theatrically effective reading of the character, for Mr Quayle succeeds in humanizing the toughness by letting something attractively boyish peep through at times.[32]

This reading is more subtle than it sounds. By electing to stress the military element (something that Kemble or Kean, say, could never have done) Quayle softened the asperities of the part. Soldiering was a shared bond between actor and audience, many of whom would have served in the war. In 1952, the military note suggested less militarism than a kind of nostalgia. The brutal CO receded into folklore. In addition, Quayle detached his Coriolanus from a simple identification with the patricians, and Kenneth Tynan confirms that the overall effect was quite sympathetic. 'Coriolanus is a militarist, a Roman Junker, sandwiched between the plebs, whom he spurns, and the patricians, whom he despises. Stratford gave the play what you might call a Tory emphasis. Coriolanus, that is to say, emerged as quite a modest chap, for all his bad temper.'[33]

Laurence Olivier's Coriolanus at Stratford in 1959 (directed by Peter Hall) is the most distinguished of our time. His previous Coriolanus (1938) suggested, for obvious reasons, an 'embryo Fascist dictator'.[34] The 1959 performance marks the shift in emphasis, in modern Coriolanuses, from political to human relationships; and I take Kitchin's judgement as the measure of a certain groundswell of our times: '. . . the play . . . revolves finally on the relationship between Coriolanus and his rival, not on the conflicts with plebeians, senators and his mother'.[35] This is central. Thus, the climax of Olivier's performance, for Kitchin, was the handshake that sealed the pact with Aufidius. Such an approach does not deny the other relationships in the play; it merely reorders priorities of emphasis. Coriolanus' relationship with his mother remains fully stated:

> Although he greeted his wife with a tender break in his voice, the scene was aligned on Volumnia in a way to prepare us for the capitulation later on. Nobody, I think, lacking knowledge of English public-school *mores* could have hit exactly this note of sulky pride, a result of the man of action's narcissism held back by the necessity to belittle success in the presence of social equals. The modesty of Marcius is false modesty, as had been obvious when Olivier writhed in discomfort at the praises heaped on him by his fellow generals, only to release a cold smile, unabashed, at the sound of his new title, Coriolanus.[36]

Olivier even exploited the latent comedy of the mother–son domination in his scenes with Volumnia. (Shaw, it is worth recalling, thought *Coriolanus* 'the greatest of Shakespeare's comedies'.)[37] But the overall effect was of terrifying concentration and power. Kitchin's phrase is telling: on Coriolanus' cursing of the plebeians, 'There was a bizarre impression of one man lynching a crowd'.[38]

Kenneth Tynan's account of the performance, oddly, does not even mention Aufidius; he finds the Volumnia relationship the key to the role. But much of his critique parallels Kitchin's, and he makes some points that bear directly upon our concerns. Peter Hall's direction he found 'straight and vigorous, with hardly any ideological slanting – a good way with a play that is best served when either everything is slanted or nothing'.[39] (This seems to me a sound judgement on the choices of presentation.) Here is Tynan's response to Olivier's concept of the character:

> Olivier understands that Coriolanus is not an aristocrat; he is a professional soldier, a *Junker*, if you like, reminiscent in many ways of General de Gaulle – a rejected military saviour who returns, after a long and bodeful silence, with an army at his back. Fully aware of the gap between Coriolanus and

the patricians he is serving, Olivier uses it to gain for the man an astounding degree of sympathy . . . he emphasizes Coriolanus the hater of phoneyness, the military man embarrassed by adulation, the awkward adult boy sickened equally by flattery and by the need to flatter. A cocky, jovial commander, he cannot bring himself to feign humility in order to become consul, and his sulky refusal to apologize to the people takes on, in Olivier's hands, the aspect of high political comedy. We cannot applaud the man, but we like him, and thus the battle of the part is half-way won.[40]

The last sentence links up with Dickins' point. Olivier solved the central problem of the part by disengaging the hero from patrician and plebeian, and by presenting him with a degree of sympathy. The great final *coup de théâtre* was then fully prepared:

> Olivier is roused to suicidal frenzy by Aufidius' gibe – 'thou boy of tears'. *'Boy!'* shrieks the overmothered general, in an outburst of strangled fury, and leaps up a flight of precipitous steps to vent his rage. Arrived at the top, he relents and throws his sword away. After letting his voice fly high in the great, swingeing line about how he 'flutter'd your Volscians in *Cor-i-o-li*', he allows a dozen spears to impale him. He is poised, now, on a promontory some twelve feet above the stage, from which he topples, to be caught by the ankles so that he dangles, inverted, like the slaughtered Mussolini. A more shocking, less sentimental death I have not seen in the theatre; it is at once proud and ignominious, as befits the titanic fool who dies it.[41]

Since 1959, no Coriolanus, to my knowledge, has approached Olivier's in acuity of analysis, brilliance, and judgement in presentation. It remains an acting peak. But the play moves still, as it must, to the rhythm of the times. Tyrone Guthrie demonstrated this, with his compelling flair, in the Nottingham Playhouse production of 1963. (One speaks of 'his' *Coriolanus*, and not the nominal lead, John Neville's.) Two features are worth noting. The production was staged in French Empire costume, a device that heightened the sense of political faction yet supplied no very precise historical analogy. The strength and the impact of the production, however, lay in its emphasis on the Coriolanus–Aufidius relationship. This was presented as a prolonged homosexual duet; and the wordless elegy that Aufidius crooned over his dead rival made startling theatre. As it happened, Ian McKellen made his first major public success as Aufidius, and this is one of the very rare occasions when the acting honours of the play went elsewhere than with the title role. Guthrie's *Coriolanus* was notable for its concentration on the drama as a private core to which the public events are related – and not as a set of political mechanisms that largely condition, and account for, the individual.

VIII

The more explicitly political elements appear, in fact, to have hived off and reconstructed themselves as free adaptations, as though the original text were not political enough. The versions of Brecht, Grass and Osborne return to the seventeenth- and eighteenth-century tradition of adapting this play. Brecht's *Coriolan*, written in 1951–2, is heavily slanted against Coriolanus, cutting many references to his nobility.

> Brecht adds lines to arouse sympathy for the plight of the Plebeians, who are neither fickle nor cowardly. Brecht invents a nameless Plebeian with a child, who appears in two scenes to suggest that the working class is building for the future. When they examine Coriolanus for the Consulship, the Plebeians are concerned with the present more than the past; Brecht invents a shipful of Volscian corn that Coriolanus refuses to distribute after his victory. The Plebs turn against the warrior because he denies them food. . . .[42]

Coriolanus is viewed as a historical and social anachronism, good only for war. There are no praises for him after his death: '*Die Offiziere des Aufidius fallen über Coriolan her und durchbohren ihn.*' Brecht adds a final scene in which Menenius makes a motion to the Senate for special commemoration of the hero, and Brutus the tribune moves that the Senate proceed with current business. The business of living, and social progress, thus takes over from a defunct type. Grass's *Die Plebejer proben den Aufstand* need only be mentioned here, since it is derivative from Brecht's version and turns on the East German uprising of 1953. Word of the uprising filters into the theatre where *Coriolan* is under rehearsal, and the central issue is the attitude of the 'Boss', the director (Brecht) towards the news. This is too far from Shakespeare to pursue.[43] John Osborne's *A Place Calling Itself Rome* (1973) is in essence a right-wing polemic, in which the central figure rails against the ills of contemporary society. It is for Osborne a variant of the system he adopts in *Inadmissible Evidence* and *Look Back in Anger*. The flavour is caught in this response of Coriolanus to banishment:

> Banish me? *I* banish *you!* Stay here in your slum. And strike. Communicate. Get shaken with rumours; fads; modishness; greed; fashion; your clannishness; your lives in depth. May you, but you won't, one minute of that depth, know desolation. May your enemies barter and exchange you coolly in their own better market-places. . . . I have seen the *future* . . . here . . . and it doesn't work! *I* turn my back. There is a world *elsewhere!*[44]

These are curiosities, testimony to the enormous vitality of the Coriolanus story. The mainstream of *Coriolanus* productions on the English stage confirms a disengagement from the nakedly political aspects of the text. The point is explicit in Irving Wardle's review of the 1967 *Coriolanus* presented by the RSC:

> John Barton's production, therefore, is the opposite of the version brought to London by the Berliner Ensemble. There is no ideological division between the masses and the nobility; all in one sense or another are equally engaged in the fight for territory. And Coriolanus – far from being a pampered patrician engaged in costly warfare to gratify his personal vanity – becomes an archetype of what Robert Ardrey has called 'territorial man'.[45]

Ardrey – whose *The Territorial Imperative* appeared in 1966 – was the peg on which to hang this interpretation; but one suspects that the production was always going to be non-political. Others confirm Wardle's impression: 'The director has avoided the fashionable temptation to read into the play a commentary on 20th century dictatorships. Coriolanus is not a political figure at all, but an aristocrat who reckons that it is his right to rule the people if he wants to. . . .'[46] The tradition of anti-heroic leads was extended. 'Instead of a great man we saw only an ordinary man coming to pieces.'[47] '. . . merely a petty patrician.'[48] Alan Brien's cameo catches this Coriolanus:

> Here Coriolanus is a glacial prefect, dedicated to an impossible code of honour, dominated by his mother, unconsciously suppressing a strong crush on a rival school-fellow, fated to break down when the antagonism between his unacknowledged passions and his boasted ideals becomes too strong.
> Ian Richardson, made up as the blond twin of Aufidius, gives a remarkable impersonation of a man who seems positively varnished under a veneer of upper-class correctness – a correctness which applies only to social equals and does not forbid the kicking, insulting, even killing of inferiors who do not understand or respect his standards.[49]

As so often in England, the rigours of the class-war yield to the pleasures of class-consciousness. But perhaps Ronald Bryden was right in detecting 'At its heart . . . a perverse sexual glamour'.[50] This is well in line with the RSC's approach to a number of texts; and the subtly erotic element in the Roman plays has not been missed by the commentators.[51] Again, we return to the preoccupation with the private core of *Coriolanus*, rather than with the political schism it appears to dramatize.

IX

That is the essence of what I take to be the contemporary approach to
Coriolanus. The major productions of the 1970s continued to illustrate
the point. The RSC's *Coriolanus* (1972), directed by a team led by
Trevor Nunn, was not acclaimed by critics or public.[52] But it was at
least interesting for the area of its emphases. The Roman crowd, once
a terrifying theatrical symbol of the proletariat on the march, had
shrivelled to a few units in a Gallup Poll. Second Citizen was clearly
identifiable as the Working-Class Tory, and First Citizen unable to
work up much passion from his associates; given their small numbers
and presence, it would have been absurd if he could. Coriolanus (Ian
Hogg), no very commanding figure, had nothing to beat. The class-
war would not take place. His major relationship, as before, was with
Aufidius, though less as a theatrical *leitmotiv* than as an *obbligato*. The
real force of the production lay in its statement of the love-affair
between the Romans and the Volscians. (This, of course, followed on
the same company's treatment of the Greek–Trojan entanglement in
Troilus and Cressida.) Aufidius and Coriolanus were locked in an inter-
tribal situation. And the Volscians – lithe, stripped, hissing between
clenched teeth – appeared as Indian braves. We have moved from
politics, through psychology, to anthropology.

The 1972 production was not well received; yet the 1973 revival,
with a recast lead, was highly successful. Nicol Williamson's
Coriolanus, commandingly tall and with an electrically intense stage
presence, transformed the production. One critic saw him as 'a fell
and fanatical Scots chieftain, stalking across the braes in search of
Papists to decapitate . . . he has more authority, more grim charisma
than Ian Hogg last year, and his anger comes across with far more
force . . .'.[53] This was a Coriolanus incapable of understanding
himself. He could not switch from soldier to statesman, and failed to
understand his mother's grip on him or his own simple incapacity to
function without Rome. The great moment of the production, as all
the critics concurred, came as he crumbled before Volumnia's Act V
appeal: 'Only once does Mr Williamson pause – and what a pause, a
single shot held longer than even Harold Pinter or John Ford would
dream could grip an audience – when his mother begs him to spare
Rome . . . "Mother . . . what . . . have . . . you . . . DONE?" the
monster cries, giving each word like a pint of blood.'[54] That con-
vulsive cry – it is on a par with Nicol Williamson's ending of *Diary of
a Madman* – remains on the record of stage history. The London
critics voted Williamson the Best Actor of the Year award for his

Coriolanus of 1973. No recent production more completely bears out
J. C. Trewin's assertion of Coriolanus: 'To win us in the theatre he
should have the power of a burning-glass; ideally he should be
charged with arson'.[55]

And finally the RSC *Coriolanus* of 1977, which, if anything, takes
farther the trends I have outlined. 'A non-political production of
Coriolanus sounds a contradiction in terms,' says Irving Wardle, 'but
Mr Hands has gone as far as it is possible to achieving one.'[56] Alan
Howard's major parts of the 1970s were built on the idea of being-as-
role-playing. His Henry V was a man learning how to play Henry;
Antony a man playing, with decreasing competence, the great
duumvir; Hamlet a man unsure how to play Hamlet. (Howard's
Rover, in *London Assurance*, was an engaging lampoon on this
approach.) Hence, his Coriolanus appeared as a man trying, and
failing, to *be* 'Coriolanus'. Benedict Nightingale saw him as 'marooned
in the heroic myths with which his vulture-mum must endlessly have
regaled him in the cot. He's Peter Pan in a leather cuirass, a giddy,
shining romantic infinitely less interested in promotion to high office
than in chivalric adventures with the local Hook.'[57] The relationship
with Aufidius, as always in modern productions, was crucial, and the
homoerotic element was plain enough: 'Both [Coriolanus and
Aufidius] are dressed in identical black leather (unfortunately, this
design trait of the RSC is looking annually less like Brechtian realism
and more like a fetish), engaged in a secret death rite of their own
devising. This is certainly a Coriolanus who spends his real honey-
moon on the fields of Corioli rather than in the bedchamber of his wife
Virgilia . . .'[58] The general feeling appeared to be that the RSC was
working out a vein of black-leather glamour, and that Howard's
striking if mannered Coriolanus was a version of what had already
been seen. At the end, the savage impact of Olivier and Williamson
was not quite present: 'With Howard's tears we are aware of a much
more abstract tragedy – a man who is failing at the last moment to
become a superman . . .'[59] All this by-passes the process of
conventional political analysis. It is curious that political theatre was
extensively mounted in the England of the 1970s, but that *Coriolanus*
was not a part of that movement.

Time resists division, but I shall lay a few categories, lightly, on the
three centuries of *Coriolanus* production we have considered. The
primitivism of the seventeenth- and eighteenth-century versions,
essays in crude and opportunistic political relevance, ended with
Kemble. His Coriolanus was a monument of neo-classic art; and the

Romantics failed to take the part over. Coriolanus, unlike Hamlet, resisted assimilation into the Romantic myth. Macready's production of 1838 I take to be the first of modern times, the first to appreciate the implications of the Roman crowd and the first to state in terms we can recognize the continuing political relevance of the conflict. That Roman crowd continued to grow, and to cast its long shadow over *Coriolanus*, into the twentieth century. The Roman plebeians co-starred with Benson, and contested with Irving himself. But, following the polarization of politics in the 1930s, the fascination with that menacing crowd has dwindled. It is understood, perhaps, that the battle has been won or, at any rate, resolved; perhaps, that there are more interesting ways of formulating a social and psychic subsidence. The contemporary era (from 1945 on, shall we say) projects Coriolanuses who are in part detached from, though in part formed by, the crude opposition of patrician and plebeian. With such Coriolanuses, the focus of interest shifts to include Rome with Corioli. The substratum of the play, that primeval layer upon which the super-structure is based, is now seen to be less the conflict of Roman with Roman than the relationship of Roman with Volscian. And that, in turn, means the relationship of man with man, with whatever emphasis of sexuality and group that the actors and directors impart. The overt politics of *Coriolanus* are muted or lost on the contemporary English stage, and what remains is the private core of being.

NOTES

1 One can chart, say, European Romanticism perfectly well through its relations with Shakespeare, on the stage as well as in the study.

2 John Palmer, *Political Characters of Shakespeare* (London: Macmillan, 1945), p. 250.

3 Ibid.

4 Details of Tate's version are given in John Genest, *Some Account of the English Stage, 1660–1830* (London, 1832), Vol. I, pp. 326–9; G. C. D. Odell, *Shakespeare from Betterton to Irving* (New York: Scribner, 1920), Vol. I, pp. 59–63; and Hazelton Spencer, *Shakespeare Improved* (Cambridge, Mass.: Harvard University Press, 1927), pp. 265–72.

5 John Loftis emphasizes that the fear of Jacobite rebellion generated a whole cluster of Shakespearean adaptations at this time: Theophilus Cibber's *Henry VI*, Lewis Theobald's *Richard II*, Buckingham's *Julius Caesar* and *Marcus Brutus*, Hill's *Henry V*, and Ambrose Philip's *Humfrey Duke of Gloucester*. John Loftis, *The Politics of Drama in Augustan England* (Oxford: Clarendon Press, 1963), p. 81.

6 John Dover Wilson notes that in Act III 'the riot in which the tribunes and plebeians were driven away was excised and the people's case thereby weakened' (New Cambridge edition of *Coriolanus* (Cambridge: Cambridge University Press, 1960), p. xlvi).

7 *The Times*, 16 December 1811 (quoted in Odell, op. cit., Vol. II, p. 104).
8 L. H. and C. W. Houtchens, *Leigh Hunt's Dramatic Criticism 1808–1831* (New York: Columbia University Press, 1949), p. 104.
9 P. P. Howe (ed.), *The Complete Works of William Hazlitt* (London and Toronto: J. M. Dent, 1933), Vol. XVIII, p. 198.
10 Ibid., Vol. V., p. 347.
11 Ibid., Vol. V., p. 348.
12 Ibid., Vol. V., p. 349.
13 Ibid., Vol. XVIII, p. 290.
14 Henry Morley, *Journal of a London Playgoer* (London, 1866), pp. 261–2. (Quoted by John Dover Wilson, p. xlvii.)
15 *The Times* could not even approve wholeheartedly of a text shorn of emendations and additions, and found the production a disappointment. See Odell, op. cit., Vol. II, pp. 150–1.
16 See Macready's *Reminiscences and Selections from His Diaries*, ed. Sir Frederick Pollock (London, 1975), Vol. I, pp. 202–3.
17 Houtchens and Houtchens, op. cit., p. 224.
18 *John Bull*, 19 March 1838. (Quoted in Odell, op. cit., Vol. II, pp. 212–13).
19 *The Times*, 14 February 1901.
20 Ibid.
21 Ibid.
22 R. Dickins, *Forty Years of Shakespeare on the English Stage* (London, 1907), p. 98. Quoted in H. H. Furness' New Variorum edition of *Coriolanus* (Philadelphia, Pa: J. B. Lippincott, 1928), p. 735.
23 *The Times*, 14 February 1901.
24 Dickins, op. cit.
25 *The Times*, 16 April 1901. (Quoted in Odell, op. cit., Vol. II, p. 456.) The programme to the RSC *Coriolanus* of 1967 suggests an additional dimension: 'An imperialist version of the play might be sensed in this picture of Henry Irving and Ellen Terry in the Lyceum Production of 1901, the year of Queen Victoria's death. The Lyceum designs were by Sir Lawrence Alma Tadema, R.A.'
26 Arthur Symons, *Plays, Acting, and Music* (London, 1909), p. 57.
27 *The Times*, 16 April 1901.
28 Dickins, op. cit., p. 98.
29 M. Stavisky, implicated in the Bayonne frauds, shot himself on 10 January 1934, when about to be arrested. The police exercised what was thought to be a suspicious tardiness in the final stages of making the arrest.
30 John Palmer, 'Coriolanus and M. Stavisky: theatre and politics in France', *The Times*, 20 February 1934, p. 12.
31 Ibid. The reader will find a detailed treatment of Piachaud's version in Ruby Cohn's *Modern Shakespeare Offshoots* (Princeton, NJ: Princeton University Press 1976), pp. 10–16.
32 *The Times*, 14 March 1952.
33 Kenneth Tynan, *Curtains* (New York: Atheneum, 1961), p. 34.
34 Laurence Kitchin, *Mid-Century Drama* (London: Faber, 1960), p. 51.
35 Ibid., p. 136.
36 Ibid., p. 137.
37 Edwin Wilson (ed.), *Shaw on Shakespeare* (New York: Dutton, 1961), p. 225.
38 Kitchin, op. cit., p. 140.
39 Tynan, op. cit., p. 240.

40 Ibid., p. 240.
41 Ibid., p. 241.
42 Cohn, op. cit., p. 18. This work (on which I have drawn throughout this paragraph) contains a detailed discussion of Brecht's version on pp. 16–21, 364–70.
43 Grass's play is discussed in Cohn, op. cit., pp. 370–4. See also Christopher Innes, *Modern German Drama: A Study in Form* (Cambridge University Press, 1979), pp. 52, 55–6, 93–5.
44 Quoted in Cohn, op. cit., p. 24.
45 *The Times*, 13 April 1967. The main point is elaborated: 'Wherever one looks the same motives are at work. Even the passive Virgilia strikes out like a wild cat when her security is threatened; and Menenius, who lives only in his possessive relationship with Coriolanus, changes from a fatherly counsellor into a spiteful old man when he is rejected by his idol.'
46 B. A. Young, *The Financial Times*, 13 April 1967.
47 Peter Lewis, *Daily Mail*, 13 April 1967.
48 Philip Hope-Wallace, *The Guardian*, 13 April 1967.
49 *Sunday Telegraph*, 16 April 1967.
50 *The Observer*, 16 April 1967.
51 See, for instance, G. Wilson Knight, 'The eroticism of *Julius Caesar*', in *The Imperial Theme* (London: Methuen, 1951), pp. 63–95; and Ralph Berry, 'Sexual imagery in *Coriolanus*', *Studies in English Literature 1500–1900*, vol. XIII (Spring, 1973), pp. 301–16.
52 Richard David discusses the production at length in *Shakespeare in the Theatre* (Cambridge: Cambridge University Press, 1978), pp. 139–49.
53 Benedict Nightingale, *New Statesman*, 2 November 1973.
54 Alan Brien, *Plays and Players* (December 1973), p. 33.
55 J. C. Trewin, *Going to Shakespeare* (London: George Allen & Unwin, 1978), p. 236.
56 *The Times*, 22 October 1977.
57 *New Statesman*, 28 October 1977.
58 Peter Ansorge, *Plays and Players* (December 1977), p. 22.
59 Ibid., p. 23.

CHAPTER TWO

Measure for Measure

The great changes in the staging of *Measure for Measure* over the last quarter of a century stem from a collective revision of judgement on the play – one shared by theatrical and academic professionals together with the general public. It was possible for the editor of a highly successful and much-esteemed work to write, in 1951: '*Measure for Measure* in spite of its touches of beauty remains one of Shakespeare's worst plays. Its badness, however, has not prevented it from having great popularity on the stage.'[1] No scholar of repute could publish such a judgement today. That text is still on sale, but David Bevington's revision of 1973 has silently erased a judgement that belongs to history. It is now universally accepted that *Measure for Measure*, whatever its difficulties, is one of the leading achievements of Shakespeare's Jacobean work.

What has happened to change the general view of *Measure for Measure?* In part, it is a movement of taste. The Problem Plays – the term is still debatable, but I use it as shorthand for *Measure for Measure, Troilus and Cressida, All's Well That Ends Well* – have found their audience. The asperities, the withholding of easy identifications from the audience, the sense of humanity gripped in complex moral predicaments – all this suits our taste well. A refusal to sentimentalize the Problem Plays permits their complexities to be scrutinized in a bleak Northern light. The result now appears as a recognition of their artistic integrity, not as Shakespeare's failure to organize a dramatic experiment. The Problem Plays have 'undergone a revaluation so radical as to amount to a rediscovery'.[2]

The progress of *Measure for Measure* since mid-century, and particularly since 1970, is a guide to the changing values of the era. The play's litmus quality depends on its final action, the staging of Isabella's response to the Duke's proposal. That is a gesture of climactic significance; it cannot be masked or elided. It defines the import of the entire preceding action. And its meaning has always to be imparted by actors who must ask themselves the only question that matters at the end: Can *this* Isabella accept *this* Duke? If not, why not? There is now no question of a routine or traditional response involving an acceptance – if anything, the practice of the 1970s has established an opposite tradition. It is with the Duke and Isabella that the special quality of recent productions must be sought, and it is on them that I concentrate.

I

Modern times begin for *Measure for Measure* with Peter Brook's classic production of 1950. This made a formidable impression, yet in retrospect appears a theatrically brilliant presentation of a view of the play current since G. Wilson Knight's *The Wheel of Fire* (1930). Brook has explained his view thus:

> . . . this ambiguity makes it one of the most revealing of Shakespeare's works – and one that shows these two elements, Holy and Rough, almost schematically, side by side. They are opposed and they co-exist. In *Measure for Measure* we have a base world, a very real world in which the action is firmly rooted. This is the disgusting, stinking world of mediaeval Vienna. The darkness of this world is absolutely necessary to the meaning of the play: Isabella's plea for grace has far more meaning in this Dostoevskian setting than it would in lyrical comedy's never-never land.[3]

Evidently, Brook found the religious thought of the play central, and projected the 'rough' world as one given significance by the 'holy'.[4] So Richard David found in the production an entire approbation of the Duke:

> If the play is to mean anything, if it is to be more than a series of disjointed magnificences, we must accept the Duke's machinations as all to good purpose, and himself as entirely wise and just. Peter Brook presented Vincentio rather as Friar turned Duke than as Duke turned Friar.[5]

This effect is in part a distortion. Herbert Weil has argued that Brook's cuts shaped the Duke into a much more consistent, 'straight' figure than the text suggests. 'Brook's prompt-books surprise us by the number of significant passages that are deleted.'[6] This is well documented, yet as one studies the prompt-book it is not clear that a major directorial motive is not an urge to clarify and simplify. It so happens that much of the Duke's language is tortuous and indirect, and 'to leave out much of the Duke's clumsy verbosity'[7] has an obvious theatrical justification. The net effect is to make the Duke 'more efficient and less the manipulator',[8] leaving out certain hints of motivation. But Isabella, too, changes subtly under this treatment. Weil does not mention the departure of 'I had rather my brother die by the law than my son should be unlawfully born', surely one of the unloveliest lines in the play. Brook's production, then, takes with the utmost seriousness the view of themselves projected by the Duke and Isabella; and protects them, so to speak, against the evidence which could jeopardize this view.

II

And this line, broadly, held up through the next two decades, as Jane Williamson's study of *Measure for Measure* demonstrates. I summarize its main points here. In the 1950s the dominant conception of Vincentio was that of model prince: wise, virtuous, authoritative. Such was the impression created by Harry Andrews in Peter Brook's production. So, also, the Duke of Anthony Nicholls at Stratford (1956) and the Old Vic (1957) under the respective directions of Anthony Quayle and Margaret Webster. 'In the early 1960s professional productions of *Measure for Measure* began, increasingly, to present the Duke as the semiallegorical, God-like figure that some theatrical reviewers had been looking for in the mid-1950s and that literary critics had been discussing since the 1930s.'[9] Tom Fleming's Vincentio in John Blatchley's production (Stratford, 1962) 'consistently impressed the critics as being a providential, Godlike character. But to some, at least, he seemed to be a God with repellent as well as attractive qualities, to be an enigmatic, mysterious deity who controlled a universe in which happiness seemed to be achieved only through pain.'[10] Michael Elliott's Old Vic production (1963) went still farther in its acknowledgement of the allegorical presence in the text. James Maxwell's Duke appeared 'a mysterious semi-divine personage' to *The Times,* and to another reviewer was invested with 'awesome saintliness'.[11] We can see the future signalled very clearly in the *New Statesman*'s reaction, however. Roger Gellert found this religiosity intolerable, and concluded:

> But when Duke Vincentio returns for his dénouement the brazen gates and everlasting doors of Malcolm Pride's set are lifted up and he steps forth with the sun for his halo, like Christ, no less, coming into his Kingdom. It came over as a moment of staggering impertinence.[12]

Providential Dukes, one detects, are under notice to quit. The allegorical treatment might seem to have reached its apotheosis in Tyrone Guthrie's production at the Bristol Old Vic (1966).

A programme note by Guthrie suggested that the play was to be given a theological interpretation not unlike that of the Old Vic production of 1963, that it was to be interpreted as a divine allegory with the disguised Duke representing the absent deity. With respect to the Duke and the various aspects of his role Guthrie wrote explicitly:

I suspect he is meant to be something more than a glorified portrait of royalty. Rather he is a figure of Almighty God; a stern and crafty father to Angelo, a stern but kind father to Claudio, an elder brother to the Provost . . . and to Isabella, first a loving father and eventually, the Heavenly Bridegroom to whom at the beginning of the play she was betrothed.[13]

All the same, the part was played against the announced grain. John Franklyn Robbins' Duke was variously described as 'puckish', 'breezy', 'sprightly', 'raffish', 'a jovially eccentric figure, whirling his crucifix like a propeller'.[14] Guthrie intended a complexity and diversity of response, and his programme-note offered a final clue:

And may we not suppose that in showing the Duke's considerable and calculated ruthlessness, as well as his wisdom and humour, Shakespeare is permitting himself a theological comment upon an all-wise, all-merciful Father-God, who permits the frightful and apparently meaningless disasters which unceasingly befall his children?[15]

Blatchley's, Elliott's and Guthrie's Dukes offered variations on the same system: they shared the view that *Measure for Measure* is allegorical, and that the Duke functions as an agent of, if he does not correspond to, God.

III

That was the received view – one might say the Establishment view – of the play. For our purposes here, the contemporary era can be thought of as starting in 1970, the terminal date of Jane Williamson's study. The seminal production, noticed at the end of her paper, was John Barton's with the RSC. This can be viewed as extending the line of inquiry observable in David Giles' production at Stratford, Ont. (1969),[16] and also as embodying a general restlessness with Godlike Dukes. In its own right, the production launched a complete theatrical re-examination of the text. The Duke became, not a quasi-religious figure, but an all-too-human, not overly competent functionary: 'In appearance, with his Holbein cap and spectacles, he suggests a university vice-chancellor: a paternal administrator, whose encouraging smiles are always contracting into icy severity.'[17] As for Isabella, a programme-note by Anne Barton supplies the vital perspective: 'Isabella's purity conceals an hysterical fear of sex which scarcely allows her to speak of her brother's fault, and leads directly to her unlovely attack upon him in prison.' And the conclusion leaves Isabella alone on stage, unresponsive to the Duke's overtures, silently resistant.

It is this conclusion, the most original single feature of Barton's production, that crystallizes the director's concept. How original may be gauged from Robert Speaight's comment: 'Mr Barton has had the brilliant inspiration of leaving her alone on the stage, unresponsive to the Duke's proposal.'[18] Speaight, a critic of rare authority, spoke from fifty years' experience of theatre, and he found Isabella's reception of the proposal a 'brilliant inspiration'. I take this to be testimony to a revolutionary departure in *Measure for Measure*'s stage history. And I add some curiously contributory evidence from critical writing. Tillyard, in his book on the Problem Plays, speaks of Isabella 'consenting to marry the Duke at the end of the play'.[19] On the following page occurs 'we must not forget that in the play Isabella marries. . .'.[20] An unlucky admonition, that. William Empson, in his classic study, actually refers to 'her decision to marry the Duke'.[21] Now, when critics of the stature of Tillyard and Empson are detected in gross error – and the same one – we can surely look for a reason beyond human fallibility in general. I suggest that, in a sense, they were not wrong. They were faithfully reporting their recollection of the play as seen. Isabellas, it seems, used always to accept the Duke's proposal. Nowadays – beginning with Barton's production – they have at least an option. I shall document this shortly; but at this point we have to ask why.

Two primary causes suggest themselves. The first concerns authority. It is a truism that the general esteem in which authority is held – political, social, institutional – has been declining in the West for some time now, certainly over the last half-generation. The idea of the all-wise, omnicompetent, Providential ruler may have reached its terminus in the reigns of Churchill and de Gaulle, Adenauer and Eisenhower. All these were widely revered by a mass public in their day. The contemporary public has diminished expectation of its rulers. It expects feet of clay, and usually finds them. Historic events often crystallize what has been happening for a long time; so it is hardly fanciful to point out that contemporary *Measure for Measure* productions began (or were conceived) shortly after *les évènements de mai*, 1968. The student revolts in Paris, together with the student manifestations in America and England, dealt deep wounds to the structures of academic authority then obtaining. In France, the students all but supplied the impetus to topple the government of the last great father-figure. I surmise, then, that these events signalled the end of an era in which the general public would take very seriously the pretensions of those in sole political authority.

The second cause, equally obvious, is the change in the position of women. Dramatized in the activities of militant feminists, and in the major legal changes in the status of women initiated in the last few years, it affects the consciousness of countless people who do not see themselves as directly concerned with the movement at all. This central theatrical fact dominates the assumptions relating to Isabella's behaviour in the final scene. In the past, it has always seemed natural and virtually inevitable for Isabella to accept the Duke's proposal. And, indeed, there is a formal historical justification for this: throughout the ages it has been enormously difficult for women to reject the advances of the Prince himself. In our time, many women have spoken of the stress on 'marriage' and 'motherhood' as the perceived goals of feminine existence in the 1950s. But today a climate of opinion exists in which these assumptions no longer hold. It appears impossible to the actress playing Isabella, and to the director who must advise her, that the truth of the part requires a serene acquiescence. The primary issue is one of personal integrity. Isabella's 'more than our brother is our chastity' is a statement that her entire selfhood is bound up with her chastity. It is not a straightforward matter of morals at all: 'chastity' is the term that sums up *her* way, *her* choice, and the Duke's brusquely public courtship is perceived as another kind of assault upon her. Simply, a contemporary actress will not perceive marriage as the automatic close to the play; and neither will the audience.

IV

These considerations I take to be the main background elements in today's productions of *Measure for Measure*. We can now sketch in some documentation. Keith Hack's production for the RSC (1974) was heavily criticized, though a case for it can be made out.[22]

Essentially it presented an extreme version of the adverse view of the Duke. Barrie Ingham played him as a posturing role-player, one intoxicated with the joys of manipulating his subjects. In a corrupt Vienna, nothing was more corrupt than the motives of the Establishment.[23] This parody of contemporary inclinations was presented without subtlety or guile, altogether lacking that ambivalence which seems to have been Shakespeare's objective in this enterprise. Nevertheless, the production appears as an ill-judged attempt to go with the grain of the times.

Two altogether superior and subtler treatments were on view in 1975. At Stratford, Ontario, Robin Phillips set the play in 1912, though at least one critic found it 'fin-de-siècle'. (These minor misconceptions of period dog the theatrical historian.) It is the Vienna of Franz-Josef and Schnitzler, with allusions to the underworld of *Dreigroschenoper*. No Godlike figure rules here:

> William Hutt is the Duke, with an eye for a housemaid's thigh, and an arm that over-comradely embraces a junior officer. Mr Hutt's performance is of especial value to the production, demonstrating that the balance of mercy and justice can only be achieved by one who has acknowledged his fallibilities.[24]

Clearly, here is a humanizing of authority, not a send-up. The same is true of Jonathan Miller's Freudian *Measure for Measure* (Greenwich Theatre), which appeared to be set in the 1920s or 1930s. (The frock coats were indeterminate, but Lucio's Fair-Isle pullover under his lounge suit could scarcely be other than interwar.) 'He has brought the action forward to the time of Freud's Vienna (backed with pastiche Schoenberg by Carl David) and localized it in a society where instinct is stifled by the code of correct behaviour: the zone, in short, of civilization and its discontents.'[25] Franz-Josef and Schnitzler are light-years away from this fallen Vienna.

> . . . the Duke is divested of divine overtones. The office he transfers to Angelo is not 'the demi-god, Authority', but a seedy room furnished with one faded portrait, a metal bin, paper clips, rubber-stamps and books of regulations. Its eight doors and one secret panel bespeak the character of the Duke.[26]

Irving Wardle follows well the clear line of Miller's interpretation:

> As other directors have realised, the key to the play is the Duke. Miller's contribution is to ask the right question about him. Not, why does he hand power over to Angelo: but what does he do after that decision?

'Here we may see,' he announces, 'if power change purpose, what our seemers be.' From that speech other productions have built the Duke into an emblem of Providence ordering human affairs. But in Joseph O'Conor's performance it leads to the exactly opposite conclusion. Mr O'Conor cuts an entirely convincing figure as elder statesman and father confessor; so convincing indeed, whether acting benevolently or with inexplicable cruelty, that realization dawns that he is the biggest seemer of the lot. At which point the moral centre drops out of the drama.[27]

The Duke is by no means unappealing. When Lucio retails his scandals (III, ii) the Duke's first reaction is to smother a laugh; he's half-embarrassed, half-delighted that he should appear such a dog to the gossips. He soon grows angry, but the amusement is disarming. At the end, as he departs looking forlornly at the photograph of himself on the wall, he appears less a fake than an authority-figure fully conscious of authority's limitations.

And now for the Isabellas of these four productions. John Barton, as we have seen, focused on an indeterminate and provisional ending. Robert Speaight saw a corrupted pride in her;[27] Jane Williamson found a shocked rejection of the proposal:

> In the last scene it seemed clear that the Duke's one true feeling was his love for Isabel . . . and although he somehow sensed it was a hopeless case, he could not help but try to win her for his bride. 'Give me your hand and say you will be mine – He is my brother too,' said the Duke. But this young Isabella simply leaped to Claudio's arms, ignoring Vincentio. After a long pause he sighed, 'But fitter time for that.' Later, trembling, he made his last bid. 'What's mine is yours, and what is yours is mine.' After a long pause of silence, he uttered a resigned, 'So,' put on his glasses, and departed with all the others, leaving a bewildered Isabella alone on stage looking out at the audience. The royal prince of the 1950s and the Godlike Duke of the 1960s had given way to a genial bumbler.[29]

Keith Hack's Isabella, tense and angrily resistant, appeared at the end as an animal trapped in the clutches of the demoniac Duke. Given the pantomime villain confronting her, she could scarcely feel otherwise, and one reviewer saw her progress as a 'slow withdrawal into complete horror and implied madness'.[30] At Stratford, Ontario, 'Martha Henry is a bespectacled Isabella, at one moment almost vomiting sexual disgust, the next caressing Claudio in a manner than suggests the nunnery is her refuge from an incestuous passion'.[31] Robin Phillips is positive that her final reaction to the Duke cannot be an acceptance, because the text does not say so; neither can it be a rejection, for the same reason. So he left Isabella alone on stage: she circles it, plainly in an agony of doubt; then again a complete circle. The circular repetitive movement expresses the anguish and bewilderment of the predicament she feels herself in.

Finally, the Isabella of the Miller version of 1975: 'Penelope Wilton plays her as a flat chested, flat footed nun in black rubber soled shoes, clutching with purple hands a nasty handbag, into which she claws for a handkerchief to scarify her raw nose.'[32] If there is a latent sexuality here (something the Phillips production had registered strongly), it has been buried a long way down.

'More than our brother is our chastity,' says Penelope Wilton, favouring the house with a hard stare. She means it. She falls on Claudio in murderous hysteria when he asks her to save him: and goes through the Mariana intrigue in a mood of icy disapproval. The way is thus prepared for an ending where the arch trickster meets the absolute puritan. At the Duke's proposal, she backs away from him in nerveless horror, plainly heading for the convent never to re-emerge.[33]

This, of the four recent productions considered, is the only one to stage an explicit rejection. It may certainly be inferred of the Barton, Hack and Phillips staging that the emotional response is negative. The director accords full weight to their doubt and sense of entrapment. But Miller staged it so that the Duke is the last figure left. Isabella, never taking her eyes off him, has already exited, as one would back away from a poisonous snake. There is no question of ambiguity here.

And this, the final position, is the measure of the enormous gap in cultural and theatrical time that separates Miller from the early Peter Brook. The prompt-book for the 1950 production contains these instructions: at 'dear Isabel', '*Isabella crosses to Duke*,' and at the final 'You all should know' '*All walk upstage . . .*'. It is a communal harmony. Marriage, reconciliation, accord – all retroactively attest the truth and worth of the transactions. Compare it with the private failures and unhealed wounds of the contemporary personae. At the end of Miller's production, nothing has been resolved beyond the continuity of government or, rather, administration. We are left with the image of the ruler as (to adapt the phrase once used of a British premier) 'the best Duke we've got'. But that is not to say very much.

Jonathan Miller's *Measure for Measure*, with its clarity of analysis and elegance of demonstration, appeared to terminate a line of inquiry, leaving the possibilities only of imitation. Ever since 1975, Isabellas have continued to express their doubts about the Duke, with varying degrees of emphasis. 'At Edinburgh (1976) she slowly stripped off veil and habit and, a potential Duchess of Vienna, moved reluctantly towards the palace of her mischievous prince. We foresaw a weary marriage.'[34] This was Stuart Burge's production for the Birmingham Repertory, and it was retained into the following year. Again, an intelligently adverse view of the Duke (Bernard Lloyd) was advanced. Irving Wardle, who praised the production for 'A most thoughtful and brilliant treatment of the text', amplifies Trewin's sense of the ending: 'Mr Lloyd plays him . . . as a kind of heavenly stage manager, rigging up arbitrary cruel situations for his own entertainment, and failing to register everything below that level. Hence Anna Calder-Marshall's horror-struck submission to her enforced marriage; not to mention the general terror he inspires.'[35] Since then, this treatment has become general. One may easily find, in the numberless reviews collected in the spring issues of *Shakespeare Quarterly*, details of productions in which Isabella refuses the Duke. It has become a late-seventies cliché of response to the text.

And yet. It would be schematically convenient to rule a line under the *Measure for Measure* of the 1970s and say: Isabellas have turned decisively against the diverse wrongs inflicted upon them by the men of the play. As it happens, the continuing flow of evidence suggests a move away from the monolith grandeur of that gesture. Barry Kyle's production (RSC, 1978) showed a most personable and appealing Duke in Michael Pennington. The Duke appeared as 'a humane and quietly curious man whom we can easily believe would give up power simply to give absolutism a trial, and it is both plausible and moving that he should react to the horrors of the repressive regime by eventually excusing all crimes committed, as it were, under experimental duress'.[36] In keeping with this approach, the comic possibilities were fully extracted. Not only did Richard Griffiths' Pompey make a hit, but Marjorie Bland's blond alcoholic Mariana also made much of that small part. The Duke's move towards a general amnesty began immediately after the interval, in what became a romp in the cornfield with the engaging Mariana. Hence the pleasure principle began its drive towards fulfilment in the conclusion. Paola Dionisotti's Isabella accepted the Duke, not at the final intimation ('Dear Isabel,/I have a motion much imports thy good'), but at the earlier 'and for your lovely sake,/Give me your hand, and say you will be mine', whereupon she unhesitatingly leaped into the arms of the Duke. 'But fitter time for that' was not, then, an admission of a *gaucherie*, a recognition that the moment had been badly chosen. It meant 'later, later'. On this reading of the text, Isabella had discovered herself, and abandoned without regret the nunnery with its coding of her identity.

One can offer various glosses on this discovery. I confine myself here to a single clue. A. C. Hamilton recounts a revealing anecdote, in a recent paper on the teaching of *Measure for Measure*: 'The response of university students is usually muted and puzzled. I wondered why this should be until an enterprising student of mine canvassed an entire women's dorm to find out how her fellow students would respond to the terms of Angelo's ransom. Some 76 percent replied with a variation of the question: "Well, what's this Angelo like?" '[37] As with Angelo, so with the Duke. Isabella's responses will depend on the man, as well as on herself. Pragmatism, too, is a principle of conduct. One surmises that Isabellas, having made their historic gesture, are now thinking the matter over; and that the actress playing Isabella will have got the point.

NOTES

1 *The Complete Works of Shakespeare*, ed. Hardin Craig (Glenview, Ill.: Scott, Foresman, 1951), p. 834.
2 Michael Jamieson, 'The Problem Plays, 1920–1970: a retrospect', *Shakespeare Survey 25* (1972), p. 1.
3 Peter Brook, *The Empty Space* (Harmondsworth: Penguin, 1972), pp. 98–9.
4 Physically, this was rendered by employing 'the pit as a lower level of the prison . . . it was somewhere down there that Barnardine lay upon his straw' (A. C. Sprague and J. C. Trewin, *Shakespeare's Plays Today: Customs and Conventions of the Stage* (Columbia, SC: University of South Carolina Press, 1971), p. 117).
5 Richard David, 'Shakespeare's comedies and the modern stage', *Shakespeare Survey 4* (1951), p. 137.
6 Herbert Weil, Jnr, 'The options of the audience: theory and practice in Peter Brook's *Measure for Measure*', *Shakespeare Survey 25* (1972), p. 30.
7 Ibid.
8 Ibid.
9 Jane Williamson, 'The Duke and Isabella on the modern stage', in *The Triple Bond: Plays, Mainly Shakespearean, in Performance*, ed. Joseph G. Price (University Park, Pa., and London: Pennsylvania State University Press, 1975), p. 159.
10 Ibid., p. 160.
11 Ibid., p. 161.
12 Roger Gellert, *New Statesman*, 12 April 1963.
13 Williamson, op. cit., in *Triple Bond*, ed. Price, pp. 161–2.
14 Ibid., p. 163.
15 Ibid., p. 163.
16 David Giles, in his 'director's notes' for *Measure for Measure*, wrote: 'In approaching the play we have tried to avoid all of the simplistic extremes in the hopes of finding and capturing the humanity with which Shakespeare illuminates every situation. In doing so we have found that the apparent discrepancies and the violent swings of mood, so objectionable to most critical opinion, are in fact organic to a drama very much to the mood of our own time.' Quoted by Arnold Edinborough, in 'The director's role at Canada's Stratford', *Shakespeare Quarterly*, vol. XX (1969), p. 444.

17 Irving Wardle, *The Times*, 2 April 1970.
18 Robert Speaight, 'Shakespeare in Britain', *Shakespeare Quarterly*, vol. XXI (1970), p. 444.
19 E. M. W. Tillyard, *Shakespeare's Problem Plays* (London: Chatto & Windus, 1957), p. 119.
20 Ibid., p. 120.
21 William Empson, *The Structure of Complex Words* (London: Chatto & Windus, 1951), p. 284.
22 See Peter Ansorge's review in *Plays and Players* (October 1974), pp. 32–3: and Peter Thomson's in *Shakespeare Survey 28* (Cambridge: Cambridge University Press, 1975), pp. 146–8.
23 Peter Ansorge, in the review cited above, coupled the production with Jonathan Miller's first version of *Measure for Measure*: 'Both productions view the Duke as the ultimate deviant of the play' (p. 32).
24 Charles Lewsen, *The Times*, 18 July 1975.
25 Irving Wardle, *The Times*, 14 August 1975.
26 Craig Raine, *New Statesman*, 22 August 1975.
27 Wardle, op. cit.
28 Speaight, op. cit., p. 444.
29 Williamson, op. cit., in *Triple Bond*, ed. Price, p. 169.
30 Ansorge, op. cit., p. 33.
31 Lewsen, op. cit.
32 Raine, op. cit.
33 Wardle, op. cit.
34 J. C. Trewin, *Going to Shakespeare* (London: George Allen & Unwin, 1978), p. 196.
35 *The Times*, 7 May 1977.
36 Peter Stothard, *Plays and Players* (August 1978), p. 32.
37 A. C. Hamilton, 'The Case of *Measure for Measure*', in *Teaching Shakespeare*, ed. Walter Edens *et al.* (Princeton, NJ: Princeton University Press, 1977), pp. 97–8.

CHAPTER THREE

Troilus and Cressida

'We find it only too lucid,' wrote Benedict Nightingale;[1] and that
appears as the modern statement on *Troilus and Cressida*. The play has
become recognizable. No one today admits to finding it difficult or
obscure, and its thrust is towards a comprehending audience. The
play's dissonances and ironies, undercutting of posturing, and acrid
view of the great – all are in accord with the contemporary sensibility.
The most openly anti-war of Shakespeare's plays, its satiric view of
the Greek and Trojan establishments poses no kind of difficulty to us.
What is perhaps its major intellectual thesis concerning the lovers –
that people exist only through relationships in time – is well understood. It is its grasp of public and private relationships that makes
Troilus and Cressida so immediate and legible.

Moreover, the treatment of Troilus and Cressida is subtly attuned
to the present. Shakespeare takes a pair of established stereotypes,
Faithful Troilus and Faithless Cressida, and permits the traditional
case to go forward on the evidence. But he also includes evidence of a
radically contradictory nature. Troilus, on this reading, finds his
reasons for abandoning Cressida (after all the talk of 'I take today a
wife'); his immediate reaction to the bad news, 'Is it so concluded?', is
suggestive, still more so his concern for his reputation ('And, my Lord
Aeneas,/We met by chance; you did not find me here'). Cressida does
her best to remain with Troilus before yielding with bitter regret to
changed circumstances. A solitary woman in a military camp needs a
protector, preferably on the staff. Calchas ('She comes to you') is not
the man for the job. And so Diomedes, in all the circumstances, is
inevitable. All this has been well argued by Joseph Papp.[2] The
feminist position, then, is completely in accord with the text, which
thus crystallizes into Cressida's 'Ah poor our sex'. The rehabilitation
of Cressida, now with some critical backing,[3] is an index to the
modern reception of the play.

I

The implications of all this for the theatre are not wholly clear. If we concentrate on the playing of Troilus and Cressida, it is not at all plain that a revisionist approach, easy in the study, secures decisive results. Troilus is a part of considerable psychological intricacy, much more so than appears. Most actors who attempt the role, to my observation, are scarcely up to it.[4] They play it as a repeat of Romeo, and cannot encompass the ways in which Troilus is responsible for the loss of Cressida. She, on the other hand, will not gain greatly in stage terms from a critical revaluation. Actresses have usually approached the role sympathetically – that goes with its grain. Thus, they will make in practice the best possible case for Cressida.[5] So the title relationship tends not to change very much on stage.

Matters go very differently with the frame for the lovers, the Greek–Trojan establishments at war. Shakespeare's edge is clear and sharp here, and the mood of the 1960s and 1970s has been receptive to anti-war and anti-Establishment satire. The stage has accepted the invitation to attack an easy target. Where Guthrie's treatment (Old Vic, 1956) was good-humouredly irreverent, Keith Hack's (for the OUDS, 1977) was contemptuously dismissive. John Barton (RSC, 1968 and 1976) discerned as the chief motif the intense sexual accord between Greeks and Trojans. *Wars and lechery* states a relationship between the armed camps, rather than the two lovers, who become a species of sub-plot. On the whole, the military and political situation has tended to interest directors, rather than the broken idyll of Troilus and Cressida.

The problems and central choices for the director fall outside the core-relationship. First, there is the question of the production metaphor. Peter Hall (RSC, 1960) accepted a costume style of the classical era, and placed the action in a sandy cockpit or arena. So did Elijah Moshinsky for the Young Vic (1976). This approach by-passes subsequent history; and there is a genuine problem of finding a historical analogue to the text's neo-mediaevalism, the obsolete chivalry of the tournament/war-game. The repetition of 'faith', 'truth', 'honour' identifies a code of defunct values. This is a nice challenge to the director, to locate the action in a past era known to have been attached to an earlier one. Guthrie saw *Troilus and Cressida* as pre-1914, an era whose values were soon to be audited by war. Jack Landau (Stratford, Conn., 1960) placed it in the American Civil War. This is an inviting analogue, since the Confederacy was deeply imbued with Walter Scott ideals of chivalry, while the more pragmatic

Federals took over a good deal of the Greek position. (However, the audience apparently found the allusions to American history somewhat distracting.)[6] John Wood (National Arts Centre, Ottawa, 1978) saw the game metaphor as fundamental: his action was played before a set suggesting stands, with the ambience of a sporting encounter. This preserved the tournament idea, but lost the war. Perhaps Peter Hall's solution remains the most inclusive.

Within the frame, there are certain points from which the action acquires a controlling perspective. Two possibilities stand out from the others: Ulysses and Thersites. Directors used to take the great 'degree' speech as the moral core of the play. Following the established critical line, which itself conformed to Tillyard's *The Elizabethan World Picture*, 'degree' was presented as the classic social ideal, and delivered with lucidity, calm and moral authority. Thus Leo McKern's Ulysses at Stratford, 1954. All that has changed. Philip Locke's Ulysses (Young Vic, 1976) was charged with an intense intellectual passion, based on a contempt for the dolts ruining the Greek war-effort. Edward Atienza's (NAC, 1978) went farther, and showed a Ulysses consumed with suppressed rage and contempt. In him appeared not the ice of cold reason, but the passionate 'pride' and 'appetite' he detected in others. Ulysses was part of the general collapse of values, not detached from it. Contemporary practice denies Ulysses the right to stand outside the drama and comment on it. (Cressida gains thereby, since the 'daughter of the game' charge cannot be taken as unchallengeable.) Thersites, then, remains the obvious choice. And he has had a deal of directorial support, though it would be a misreading of the text to take him unequivocally as the choric voice. Barton gave him prominence, and left him on stage at the end. Hack made him Prologue/Chorus, a rigid but effective treatment which imposed a hard direct line on the production. Other possibilities – Pandarus, Diomedes and Agamemnon, for instance, are theoretically available – have not attracted directors. My impression is that they see the choice of perspective as lying between Ulysses and Thersites, and find the latter exercising a stronger pull.

II

In the discussion of postwar productions that follows, I take the prompt-text as the point of departure. This is a long play, by canonical standards, and does not contain much action. It is pre-eminently a 'talk' play. We should expect, therefore, the play to be more heavily cut in the past than today. Length, allied to a strong verbal emphasis, is no longer the handicap it used to be. A generation which accepts Shaw easily (and does not complain, as in his lifetime, that his plays are 'all talk') is not going to be impossibly stretched by *Troilus and Cressida*. We can reasonably assume that a contemporary director will have a greater confidence in the text than was possible a generation ago.

Support for this assumption is forthcoming from the first two postwar productions at Stratford. Anthony Quayle's 1948 production tampered with the text to an extent surprising today. The 'degree' speech of Ulysses, always a touchstone to the director's intentions, is cut very heavily, some twenty-three lines only remaining. The ending, again, is significantly cut. Pandarus' epilogue vanishes, leaving Troilus to end on 'Hope of revenge shall hide our inward woe'. This is the 'Romantic' way of ending the play, and the prompt-book confirms the speculation: on 'inward', Aeneas and the Trojans exeunt, and the directions call for 'lights, music', with 'on high violin note, Lights 42 IN BLACKOUT, FAST CURTAIN'. This is typical of late forties theatre (the period of, for example, Cocteau's *The Eagle Has Two Heads*), a heroic, gestural conclusion.

The Stratford production of 1954, in which Quayle moved to Pandarus and Glen Byam Shaw directed, expressed the established view of what was considered possible in the immediate postwar era. Setting and costumes were straightforwardly classical, and a leading romantic actor, Laurence Harvey, played Troilus. (During this period he also played Romeo, on stage and on film.) The prompt-book text is interesting for its cautiously optimistic view of what the audience could take. Prologue is uncut, and there are reasonable light cuts in the early encounters. The acid test, the 'degree' speech, shows cuts of only 7½ lines. The Helen scene (III, i) is uncut, and the Trojan council scene, like its Greek counterpart, is left largely intact. Again, Ulysses' 'Time hath, my lord, a wallet at his back' is a severe test of the audience, but only 2½ lines go (the image of the 'gallant horse' being 'trampled on'). So far the impression we receive, of a respectable attempt to play the text, is favourable. It is a disappointment to find the later stages less than adequately treated. The climax of the discovery scene is Troilus' outburst against 'bifold authority', and much of this goes. The cuts include Troilus' 'Think, we had mothers' to Thersites' 'Will he swagger himself out on's own eyes?' (V, ii, 144–52). The philosophic crux is 'This is, and is not, Cressid': it is very remarkable for this to go.

The conclusion, again, shapes up a romantic gesture. The final

Pandarus speech, from 'hence brother lackey, ignomy and shame' to 'sweet notes together fail', has been tacked on to the end of V, iii. This is an acceptable piece of theatrical engineering, in view of the irregularities of the original text, but it makes the play end on a note quite different from Shakespeare's design. For now the ending, as in the 1948 production, is on Troilus' 'Hope of revenge shall hide our inward woe', at which, to a despondent trumpet, all the Trojans exeunt save Troilus, who is left outlined against the walls of the doomed city. On this Richard David comments: 'But this was pure anti-climax after Pandarus' blow in the face; the play trailed off on an unresolved discord; the audience shifted uneasily, wondering if there was more to come, and departed feeling somehow cheated.'[7] All in all, the production seems an intelligent attempt to grapple with the play, yet one that does not face up fully to the bleakness and discordance of the text. 'In short, the cynical voice was shushed down, and the Virgilian allowed to speak out'[8] – a verdict perhaps owing much to the quality of Leo McKern's Ulysses. Perhaps this production came at a difficult point in theatrical time, between the romantic and gestural late forties and the harsher, modernist late fifties.

III

The new turning is clearly visible in Tyrone Guthrie's production of two years later (1956) at the Old Vic. As it happens, this preceded by three months the first night of *Look Back in Anger*, universally regarded as the trumpet heralding the contemporary era on the English stage. But there are many piquancies and surprises in Guthrie's *Troilus*. To begin with, he is utterly disrespectful of the text. There is no question of trusting the audience to follow Shakespeare's words. Prologue vanishes, and the Greek council scene suffers heavy losses: 'degree' loses a total of forty lines. This wilful cutting continues into the Trojan council, where, for instance, Troilus' vital question 'What's aught, but as 'tis valued?', together with the twenty lines following, disappears. It would seem intellectually essential to retain the sense of a formal debate on 'value' here, focused on Troilus' question. The Helen scene is allowed to run uncut following the elimination of the first forty lines (including the dialogue with the servant), and the love scene between Troilus and Cressida is given full weight, only some twenty lines disappearing. (These include Troilus' 'What too curious dreg' image, III, ii, 70, which directors habitually found obscure or dispensable.) Guthrie, having saved considerable time through his earlier excisions, now grants full space to Ulysses' 'Time hath, my lord . . .', from which only the last 2½ lines are absent. The bitter Diomed–Paris exchange is given in full, and the parting is virtually uncut. The Greek-camp episodes in Act IV show considerable winnowing, for instance in Ulysses' praise of Troilus, the courtly Hector–Ajax praise, and Agamemnon's fine speech of welcome, 'What's past and what's to come . . .' (IV, v, 163–71). The effect is to drain off the genuine chivalry of the scene. (And this, naturally, accords with the prominence given to Thersites and his view of the action.)

Guthrie's policy of condensing the purely intellectual appeal of the text is visible in the discovery scene. As in Glen Byam Shaw's production, there is a central cut in the 'This is, and is not, Cressid' outburst: it runs from 'O madness of discourse' to 'Ariachne's broken woof to enter' (V, ii, 142–52). But thereafter the cutting is fairly light, though we should note that Thersites' comment on Patroclus disappears: 'Patroclus will give me anything for the intelligence of this whore: the parrot will not do more for the almond than he for a commodious drab' (V, ii, 189–91). Presumably this is because the text here suggests Patroclus to be bisexual, whereas the production presents him as homosexual only. The fighting has some necessary cuts, and the modern-dress production obliges Guthrie to amend 'Sagittary' to 'artillery' (V, v, 14). 'Armour' references have to go, for the same reason. Interestingly, 'And *stickler*-like the armies separates;' (V, viii, 18) is changed to '*umpire*-like'. The suggestion here is of a war-game, *les grandes manoeuvres* which have changed to the real thing. The Thersites–Margarelon encounter goes – it has little relevance to the mode of this play – and half of Troilus' last-scene rhetoric; but the final address by Pandarus is intact, lacking only the obscure 'galled goose of Winchester' couplet, which is meaningless today.

In sum, the cutting is very free: it is quite wrong for John Dover Wilson to speak in the New Cambridge edition of Tyrone Guthrie 'cutting nothing but the Prologue'.[9] The general effect is to lighten the emphasis on the purely verbal and intellectual qualities of the text, and to enable *Troilus and Cressida* to be played for movement, spectacle and character-interest. The conclusion, Pandarus' address (allotted to the most accomplished actor in the cast, Paul Rogers), is a formal signal that the anti-romantic possibilities in the text have been acknowledged (though Ulysses' 'daughter of the game' reference to Cressida, IV, v, 54–63, a powerful adverse perspective on the female lead, disappears). It is, however, in the setting and characterization that the meaning of Guthrie's production must primarily be sought.

The tradition of playing *Troilus and Cressida* in classical garb is here abandoned, and the setting is European, a few years before the First World War. The Trojan officers have been seen variously as 'genial dissolute Ruritanians'[10] and as 'hard-drinking sprigs in a Hussar mess'.[11] The general impression is of Edwardian English in Troy, and this comprehends Pandarus as 'an elderly fribble in an Ascot outfit'[12] and Cressida in riding-habit. The Greeks are projected, in the main, as Kaiser Wilhelm's Germans ('arrogant Uhlans').[13] Ulysses is clearly recognizable as Admiral Tirpitz, and the monocled Menelaus resembles 'a desiccated Erich von Stroheim'.[14] The Greek expedition is a combined operation, and their rank and file are dressed as matelots. However, Achilles wears slacks, white shirt open to the waist, and a beach robe.[15] His life-style proclaims him a dropout from the Junker caste, and his pathic (Patroclus) confirms the effect. Clearly, we have strong sense of period here, and this provides further opportunities for telling castings. Helen is an Edwardian chorus-girl married into the peerage. The piano in her and Paris' apartment, together with champagne, ice-bucket and glasses, establishes the glamour (and vapidity) of the role. Thersites is a war correspondent, constantly setting up his box camera on a tripod. This brings out the voyeurism, together with the radical discontent of the man (T. C. Worsley found him 'a disgruntled Shavian radical').[16] Cassandra is a 'half-crazy dévotée of séances, in sack tunic, much embroidered, and waist-long strings of beads'.[17]

What this period flavour imparts, setting aside the succession of tactical opportunities, is a sense of the profound historical analogy. English and Germans, locked together in their long historic conflict, are the Trojans and Greeks of this century. It may not be an analogue to persuade the historian, but for the general audience there is enough truth in it to establish the production's credentials. It was, however, widely written off by the critics as 'an irreverent lark' and 'Pandarus on Ice' (or, in the *Spectator*'s heading, 'Kiss Me Cressida'), which was somewhat less than its deserts. The critical consensus seems located in Richard David's 'Though it was an amusing evening, it was also an infuriating one'.[18] And a defence of Guthrie has to take up David's 'It was a pity to place this play, of which a main subject is war, in a period that emphasized only war's glamour and never its reality'.[19] But surely war's 'glamour' is, in fact, coded in the faded chivalry that constantly emerges from the text? The appeals to a pseudo-mediaeval courtly value-system, together with Troilus' rather passé Petrarchianism, generate an ideology of unreality. It is not dissimilar to the negative qualities that we associate with 'Georgian' poetry – the qualities that found their sharpest criticism in the poetry of 1917 and 1918. That is what makes *Troilus and Cressida* 'a lament for an old world lost',[10] in the words of J. C. Trewin's review of a later production, and which responds so well to the Edwardian ambience of 'honour'.

IV

The *Troilus and Cressida* directed by Peter Hall and John Barton at Stratford (1960) clearly belongs to the modern era, if it does not inaugurate it. This was the opening year of Peter Hall's reign over the RSC, and the production exhibits the hallmarks of the Company style over the period: a cool intelligence and contemporary sensibility playing over the text, an awareness that modernity and 'relevance' would always be there and would always be necessary, a respect for the full text. It is a slight exaggeration for Robert Speaight to say that 'the plays are given practically uncut',[21] but a study of the prompt-book shows the cuts to be sparing and well thought out. The impression is of a text which has been judiciously thinned, or slimmed, rather than subjected to surgery. The Prologue stays; there are very light cuts in the opening scenes; the Greek council scene take a few reasonable cuts, but 'degree' survives virtually intact, losing only the two lines beginning 'Insisture, course, proportion . . .'. Similarly, the Trojan council suffers only moderate cuts distributed between Hector and Troilus. The essential points are made. The Helen scene is intact, and 'Time hath, my lord . . .' is uncut. The discovery scene is given full value, being almost entirely uncut: Troilus mysteriously loses four lines that other directors have taken exception to, 'O madness of discourse . . . Without revolt . . .' (V, ii, 142–6), but 'This is, and is not, Cressid' survives. The epilogue is retained in full, not even the obscure 'Winchester' couplet suffering the knife. All in all, this is a production that takes the text as seriously, within the time-limitations of performance, as it well could.

Peter Hall has always believed in the 'natural' (Renaissance, or classical or mediaeval) setting for Shakespeare, and *Troilus and Cressida* illustrates this approach. 'Mr Hall has had the startlingly original idea of letting his actors look like Greeks and Trojans . . . he evidently felt that the play was so modern that its modernity could be left to look after itself – which it very capably did.'[22] The setting was 'A bloodshot backcloth, more than a little reminiscent of Graham

Sutherland, and a sort of octagonal boxing-ring'.[23] This 'sandy cockpit'[24] won general praise, as allowing undistracted attention to be focused on to this remarkably combative action. The drama thus presented was without eccentricity of design, and permitted the actors to establish their natural roles. While the casting was not universally strong, there was praise for the lucid and intelligent Ulysses of Eric Porter. Max Adrian was consistently praised for his voyeurist Pandarus: A. Alvarez, indeed, found him 'the one focus of aroused, indulgent, and corrupt impotence for the whole play'.[25]

In all, this production won high marks for intelligence and respect for the text, if not invariably for the acting and quality of verse-speaking. J. C. Trewin found in it 'a truth that terrifies. Nothing here is mitigated, turned to favour and to prettiness.'[26] '*Troilus and Cressida* is not a play on which one ever feels the last word has been spoken; but Mr Hall's commentary will not easily be bettered' was Robert Speaight's verdict.[27] Alan Brien, under the tendentious heading 'Eden's War', saw in the production a well-founded condemnation of the leadership of both sides. 'So it is enormously to the credit of the Stratford production by Peter Hall and John Barton that these double-meanings and modern parallels strike home much more keenly than they did in Tyrone Guthrie's Old Vic version set in Edwardian costume.'[28] Here is a reaction that helps us to look for the right areas of this production's importance: style and meaning. The style is cool, hard-edged, non-eccentric, directed at eliciting inner truth however bleak. The meanings emerge always from modernity and parallelism, but are permitted to form without stridency and undue directorial underlinings. The judgement is that *Troilus and Cressida* is already a play for our times.

V

And that I take to be a received axiom of the contemporary approach to *Troilus and Cressida*. Here is Benedict Nightingale's induction to his review of John Barton's RSC production of 1968:

> *Troilus and Cressida* is the one Shakespeare play that the eternal Professor Kott hardly needed to write about, because it is the one Shakespeare play that, almost undistorted, embodies his view of life. Past ages found it bewildering, offensive or ridiculous, an affront to every Aristotelian virtue; we find it only too lucid. Where else in our literature do we get so sustained an assault on the romantic values, honour, military glory, 'pure' love? Indeed, the play goes further than this, and calls the whole concept of an

established and orderly social system into question. Self-willed and reckless
of 'degree', its people seem about to stumble over the brink into what
Shakespeare would regard as anarchy and confusion. The moral pragmatism
is tempered with a certain, inevitable, conservatism; but it's still very much
a play for an anxious generation in a pluralist society . . .'[29]

With this, as I take it, critics and general public are in substantial
agreement, though not all would phrase it so provocatively. First,
though, to the prompt-text of Barton's production. As one would
expect, it is similar to that used in the production for which he was
jointly responsible, with Peter Hall, eight years earlier (a production
that several critics invoked, to the disparagement of the later version).
It is not, however, identical, and the minor changes are interesting.
Prologue remains, and the Greek council scene is very similarly
rendered, 'degree' losing the same two lines. But there is a slight bias
towards cutting in the later version. 'Time hath, my lord' now loses
three lines, and the chivalrous exchanges between Greeks and Trojans
are diminished, as in IV, i, while the brutality of the encounter
between Diomedes and Paris is preserved uncut. More important, the
parting scene of the lovers takes a substantial cut, from Troilus' 'Nay,
we must use expostulation kindly' to Cressida's 'O Heaven! "be true"
again!' (IV, iv, 60–76). The effect is to drain off some of the intensity
of the parting and, indeed, to weaken the focus on the lovers. The
same effect is observable in a significant extension of a cut in the
discovery scene: Barton cuts, as before, the four lines beginning 'O
madness of discourse', but goes on to exclude the rest of the line
(which Hall had preserved) 'This is, and is not, Cressid'. It is difficult
to conceive the point of jettisoning this most famous of the lines
crystallizing the intellectual drama. Unsurprisingly, the Pandarus
epilogue stays in full, saving only the 'Winchester' couplet. But here,
too, is a change: Thersites has entered at the same time as Pandarus,
and after Troilus' 'Pursue thy life, and live aye with thy name', the
stage direction reads: '*Troilus (pushes Pandarus to floor) exit u/p*'.
Thersites then remains on stage at the close, and his presence
amplifies and intensifies the bitterness projected by Pandarus.

The implications of the prompt-text are realized in the *mise-en-scène*
and costumes, themselves reflecting Barton's concept. Robert
Speaight epitomizes the drift: 'Where Peter Hall emphasizes the wars
. . . Mr Barton went to town on the lechery.'[30] The change of
direction is more apparent in the costumes than in the *mise-en-scène:*
there is 'a Greek prologue, posed as on a painted vase, masked,
cloaked and helmeted in scarlet. The harsh lighting, the brilliant-
white cockpit and the black emptiness beyond remain the same.' But

'Take . . . the minute, coquettish, pleated kilts, worn like cake frills round the waist by the Greek and Trojan princes: the fashion for bare bottoms, which caused such excitement when the *Marat/Sade* was seen on Broadway, has been gaining ground rapidly on the London stage in recent months and is by no means over yet'.[31] The great love affair of this production is not Troilus and Cressida, but the Greeks and Trojans. It is expertly mounted: 'Barton handles this inner world of courtly intrigue as well as he does his outer world of oiled bodies in conflict on bare sand against a black sky.'[32] But another reviewer deplored the 'ornate vulgarity'[33] of the frequent presence of copulation in mime and sound. Achilles (Alan Howard) is presented as an effeminate, if intense and commanding, homosexual who at one point 'dressed in drag is making eyes at Hector'.[34] Speaight thought this a complete error: 'it is an elementary mistake to imagine that because a man is homosexual, he cannot at the same time be apparently, and even aggressively, masculine. Besides, Achilles was just as interested in Polyxena as he was in Patroclus – so I didn't think the transvestite charade really made sense.'[35] Setting aside the controversy as to over-done stage business, it is plain that the director has a genuine concept to project:

> Barton puts a particular, and peculiarly original, gloss on his familiar catchphrase, 'nothing but wars and lechery'. This war, he suggests, is a sort of lechery itself. War is sex and sex is war. Cressida destroys Troilus, and the Trojans meet the Greeks like lovers, almost naked, agog for the dark orgasmic flutter of killing or being killed. It is a striking and daring aperçu, more suited (one would think) to Genet than Shakespeare, but the text does seem to sustain it. The men in this play are always embracing and talking of death. 'No man alive can love in such a sort/The thing he means to kill more excellently,' says Aeneas of Diomed as, typically, they touch. The language is sensuous, cloying. 'I have a woman's longing,' cries Achilles, 'An appetite that I am sick withal/To see great Hector.'[36]

The rest of the cast illustrate or reinforce this concept. Thersites – who, as we have noted, shares the last word with Pandarus – is especially repellent. 'Few stage spectacles have been more hideous than Norman Rodway as the moulting, suppurating Thersites: he looks like an ape escaped from Porton.'[37] Similarly, the lovers have to accept a diminution of stature. The overall conception 'draws attention to itself at the expense of Troilus and Cressida themselves' was Nightingale's verdict.[38] This, from an especially well-placed and sympathetic critic, is a significant admission of the drawbacks of the production. Here is the amplification:

Troilus, in particular, should be the protagonist in more than title. It is his romantic illusions, erotic and military, that take the sharpest blows. It is he who is slowly educated in despair; he who carries the meaning of the play and gives it its shape. Without a strong and solid Troilus to invoke suicide and rail on the heavens, the ending must, as it does here, lose impact. Michael Williams is a nice enough young fellow and would make a good Romeo; but where is the depth, the intensity of feeling when, say, he asks for 'swift transportance to those fields/Where I may wallow in the lily-beds/ Proposed for the deserver'?[39]

This accords with the *Spectator*'s judgement:

Not that this Troilus – played with extreme perversity by Michael Williams as a baffled Lost Boy from *Peter Pan* – is in any position to make much of his humiliation at Cressid's hands . . . And once we have seen him bury his head in Ulysses' lap at a moment when the play's rhythm, not to mention his own words, demands a mood of hard and adult savagery – once this turning point is muffed, no wonder if the battle scenes seem a trifle desultory.[40]

The main lines of the production are now apparent. The critics, clearly, reacted with differing degrees of sympathy: in general, Hilary Spurling's condemnation of the Company's 'ornate vulgarity' and 'decorative decadence' was not shared. But the transference of interest away from the lovers to the rest of the dramatis personae, and the very heavy emphasis on corporate sexuality (one critic found the truce an 'inter-army love-in') bought a striking impression at a certain cost. The poignancy, the bruised idealism, the sense of a 'lament for an old world lost' – all this has vanished in the presence of an obsession with corrupt appetite. Thersites, always a cast member in standing, has taken over.

VI

Barton's *Troilus and Cressida* remained the last word (on the major English-speaking stage) for several years. After 1969 no important version was mounted in London, or in any of the Stratfords, until 1976; and then several interesting productions appeared within a brief space. I touch lightly on their characteristics.

The Barton version was revived in 1976, with a new casting, and the programme states its emphasis concisely. On the cover, in letters of red, appears: 'All the argument is a cuckold and a whore'; so the production stood solidly behind Thersites. Since his view of Cressida is 'A proof of strength she could not publish more,/Unless she said "My mind is now turned whore" ', it follows that she is presented unsparingly and unsentimentally. Francesca Annis played her 'mainly on two notes. One is the assured sexual specialist whom Ulysses instantly recognizes. The other is gravely reflective and still, demonstrating from the start that she knows herself well enough to realize that she is not to be trusted.'[41] She was dressed as a courtesan for her entrance to the Greek camp. The main emphasis, as in the 1968 version, was placed on the Greek–Trojan situation, with its intensity of homoerotic charge. Ulysses (Tony Church) was solidly competent, but not the hub of the drama. (One critic noted that as he approached 'Appetite, an universal wolf', he rubbed his stomach as if suffering from indigestion.[42]) A doll – icon of Cressida, Helen, or womanhood – was introduced, and the conclusion went thus:

'In desperation, he [Pandarus] dons a hideous rubber death mask, executes a *danse macabre*, and descends into a grave-like vault which, when closed, reveals Thersites, carrying a life-sized doll.'[43] This is an interestingly Brechtian device. The doll forces the audience to revalue the whole idea of 'exploitation', the more so as Cressida was not played for obvious sympathy. The doll aside, little that was new emerged, and the reviewers considered the production a reprise, displaying the same merits and subject to the same limitations as before. The most penetrating criticism came from John Elsom:

> What has been lost, of course, by this approach is Shakespeare's balancing appreciation of the chivalric code, which, however bloody and hypocritical it may have seemed to Thersites, was real enough to the better breed of knight, such as Hector. . . . By not taking the code seriously, Barton reduced *Troilus and Cressida* to a bitchy, fatalistic work, neither comedy nor tragedy, just opinionated gloom. It is ironic to reflect that this used to be the image of *Troilus and Cressida*, conveyed through the puritanical writings of Victorian critics, whose malign interpretations of the play required the John Barton of the Sixties to contradict.[44]

It is certainly possible, on the evidence of the text itself, to take the chivalric elements as a farce. But then the play's inner gyroscope is disturbed, and the drama functions as a brutal demolition of *all* values – and nothing else.

That was the approach of Keith Hack in the production he directed for the OUDS (1977). The drama's emblem was Helen (Jill Foot), who remained visible throughout, suspended above the action save for III, i, when she was lowered for her single scene. Helen, swinging languorously and preening herself in a looking-glass, was the constant reminder that the war was fought for *this*. She, then, was an image of vapidity and triviality; confronting her was Thersites, whom the director promoted as Prologue/Chorus and spokesman for the war's losers. Thersites (played by Tim McInnerny, a figure of great presence) was a wounded soldier, limping along with a combined bandage and crutch slung under one leg. His face twitched constantly, with a suggestion of shellshock. He was on stage for much of the time, including the amour of Troilus and Cressida. There was never a chance that the romance could be taken seriously, and the force of the production was directed against the military establishments. Hack's implacably Brechtian approach worked well within its chosen limits. There were some entertaining moments in the Greek council, for instance, with Agamemnon, seated with his knees up and biting his nails in schoolboy fashion, snatching up the camp gazette to read it at 'Pride is his own glass, his own trumpet, his own chronicle'. *Glass* was a stage emblem for the action. But the attack ran out of steam before the end, for V, ii (the discovery scene), is too big to mask, and Troilus and Cressida *matter*.

Troilus and Cressida, then, appear to have lost some standing of recent years. And so has Ulysses, who (as already noted) generated distinguished performances at the Young Vic (1976) and in Ottawa (1978), which were notable for their fire and intellectual passion but which were not allowed to dominate the play.[45] The action is seen as a moral anarchy; and, if anyone has the credentials to comment on it, he is Thersites.

Very broadly, then, the immediate postwar productions of *Troilus and Cressida* derived a shudder from the spectacle of lost illusions; audiences of that era evidently felt that illusions were worth having to lose. The drama of Troilus and of Cressida was given full value. A starker, bleaker view was manifest in Hall's 1960 production. It presented a world in which the lovers were simply a part of a decaying value-system everywhere apparent. The hard inclusiveness of Hall's approach did, however, ensure that all elements in the play should be projected with a sense of inner balance; thus, though the emphasis was moving away from Troilus and Cressida, they still retained their place in the design. We can best regard Barton's production, and revival, as having relegated the lovers to a species of sub-plot. Since theirs is a straightforwardly heterosexual affair, they represent a banality in the statement Barton makes. In seeing *appetite* as the key, he does indeed follow the text, but the focus has swung away from Troilus and Cressida towards the wider range of self-gratification identifiable in the Greek and Trojan communities. This inversion of production – the metaphorical becomes the literal, so to speak – makes for a fascinating but extreme and unrepeatable statement. It is, in any case, debatable as to whether it is sound policy to actualize intensively the metaphors in the text.

Above all, the productions we have considered constitute a continuing critique of Ulysses' speech on 'degree': that is always the hub of a production. Thirty years ago it was always taken seriously. Tillyard's *The Elizabethan World Picture*, a book for which 'degree' is the supreme illustration, was in academic circles as in theatrical accepted as stating the representative Elizabethan ideal of an ordered society. So 'degree' was the norm, and the events in the play a departure from it. On purely tactical grounds – the supposed attention-span of the audience – it was of course acceptable to cut the speech down, but this was no different from Kemble's rationale in his projected version of *c.*1800.[46] Today things go differently. As a general principle, we incline to accept William Empson's dictum: 'the idea that everyone held the same opinion at a given date, "the opinion of the time", is disproved as soon as you open a history book and find a lot of them killing each other because they disagreed'.[47] More specific to *Troilus and Cressida*: just as academics are now ready to read 'degree' in context as a stratagem, not a credo, so directors decline to regard it as the moral centre of the drama. The centre will not hold. What remains is a centrifugal human universe or, rather, a world of humanity seeking each other only to slake its appetite. The action of *Troilus and Cressida* is compounded of individual and communal moral solipsism. Barton's productions represent a terminus of the thought-line of the 1960s, and perhaps an absolute terminal point. It remains for directors to rediscover the play's title.

NOTES

1 Benedict Nightingale, *New Statesman*, 16 August 1968.

2 Joseph Papp, 'Directing *Troilus and Cressida*', in *The Festival Shakespeare 'Troilus and Cressida'* (New York: Macmillan, 1967).

3 See, for instance, R. A. Yoder, ' "Sons and daughters of the game": an essay on Shakespeare's *Troilus and Cressida*', *Shakespeare Survey* 25 (1972), pp. 11–25; Grant L. Voth and Oliver H. Evans, 'Cressida and the world of the play', *Shakespeare Studies*, vol. VIII (1975), pp. 231–7.

4 I have seen seven. J. C. Trewin's view was 'The lovers themselves are a perpetual challenge' (*Birmingham Post*, 18 August 1976).

5 Not invariably: see the account of Francesca Annis' Cressida for the RSC (1976). It is interesting that Papp found difficulty in inducing his actor to take an unsympathetic view of Troilus: Papp, op. cit., pp. 32–3.

6   Claire McGlinchee, 'Stratford, Connecticut, Shakespeare Festival, 1961', *Shakespeare Quarterly*, vol. XII (1961), pp. 419–23.
7   'Stratford 1954', *Shakespeare Quarterly*, vol. V (1954), p. 392.
8   Ibid., p. 390.
9   *Troilus and Cressida*, ed. John Dover Wilson (Cambridge: Cambridge University Press, 1957), p. liv.
10 Brian Inglis, *The Spectator*, 13 April 1956.
11 T.C. Worsley, *New Statesman*, 14 April 1956.
12 Ibid.
13 Inglis, op. cit.
14 Ibid.
15 These and other details are confirmed in the production file at the Old Vic.
16 Worsley, op. cit.
17 Richard David, 'Drams of eale', *Shakespeare Survey 10* (1957), pp. 130–1.
18 Ibid. p. 131.
20 *The Illustrated London News*, 6 August 1960.
21 Robert Speaight, 'The 1960 season at Stratford-upon-Avon', *Shakespeare Quarterly*, vol. XI (1960), p. 446.
22 Ibid, p. 451.
23 Ibid.
24 J. C. Trewin, *The Illustrated London News*, 6 August 1960.
25 A. Alvarez, *New Statesman*, 30 July 1969.
26 Trewin, op. cit.
27 Speaight, op. cit., p. 452.
28 *The Spectator*, 29 July 1960.
29 *New Statesman*, 16 August 1968.
30 *Shakespeare Quarterly*, vol. XIX (1968), p. 374.
31 Hilary Spurling, *The Spectator*, 16 August 1968.
32 Nightingale, op. cit.
33 Spurling, op. cit.
34 Ibid.
35 Speaight, op. cit.
36 Nightingale, op. cit.
37 D. A. N. Jones, *The Listener*, 15 August 1968.
38 Nightingale, op. cit.
39 Ibid.
40 Spurling, op. cit.
41 Irving Wardle, *The Times*, 18 August 1968. David Zane Mairowitz found that Annis 'skirts the problem of her own turnabout, moving from virtue to its opposite without apparent transition' (*Plays and Players* (October 1976), p. 21). Kenneth Hurren dismissed her as 'such a shallow, giggly minx that her behaviour is rarely startling, her fate excites little concern, and the unfortunate Troilus (Mike Gwilym), despite his putting on quite a show of misery and anguish in his betrayal, seems merely a ninny to have taken her so seriously' (*The Spectator*, 28 August 1976).
42 John Elsom, *The Listener*, 26 August 1976.
43 Frank Marcus, *Sunday Telegraph*, 22 August 1976.
44 Elsom, op. cit.
45 In a generally critical review, Sally Emerson found that 'Elijah Moshinsky's direction does not back up Ulysses' analysis. We do not see the universal wolf appetite on the rampage' (*Plays and Players* (September 1976), p. 32). With John

Wood's production, however, 'The symbolism is all too clear. War is mindless exertion and works up to something approaching a brutal sexual perversion. In a way, this can be justified by the bitter explanation of Thersites: "Lechery, lechery; still, wars and lechery: nothing else holds fashion" ' (Richard Eder, *The New York Times*, 26 January 1978). But a comic, overindulged Thersites spoilt the analysis. Someone in the cast of *Troilus and Cressida* should look as if he knew what was going on, and as if the director were backing him.

46 'Gentleman thought the degree speech "too long, and too redundant"; Kemble reduced it by forty-five percent' (Jeanne T. Newlin, 'The darkened stage: J. P. Kemble and *Troilus and Cressida*', in *The Triple Bond: Plays, Mainly Shakespearean, in Performance*, ed. Joseph G. Price (University Park, Pa., and London: University of Pennsylvania Press, 1975), p. 193.

47 William Empson, 'Mine eyes dazzle', *Essays in Criticism*, vol. XIV (1964), p. 86.

CHAPTER FOUR

Henry V

Few plays in the canon, if any, have turned around so markedly and abruptly as *Henry V*. It used to be a straightforward nationalist statement, the military epic of the English-speaking people. One could dislike the central figure, certainly. 'A very amiable monster', thought Hazlitt.[1] Shaw was harsher: 'One can hardly forgive Shakespeare quite for the worldly phase in which he tried to thrust such a Jingo hero as his Henry V down our throats. The combination of conventional propriety and brute masterfulness in his public capacity with a low lived blackguardism in his private tastes is not a pleasant one.'[2] But no one seriously questioned the play's import. Only in comparatively modern times have doubts about the play itself surfaced.[3] Gerald Gould was, I believe, the first to challenge the traditional understanding of the play: 'None of Shakespeare's plays is so persistently and thoroughly misunderstood as *Henry V* . . . *The play is ironic*' (my italics).[4] Written in 1919, Gould's reaction was obviously that of a generation whose values were transformed by the First World War. It pointed the way for the later critics who have elaborated the ironies and reservations latent in *Henry V*,[5] and who have accordingly speculated that Shakespeare's views on war correspond rather closely to their own.

This unsurprising conclusion is shared by many today. In terms of general audience response, the old, uninhibited revelling in the French débâcle is no longer possible. A traditional *Henry V* runs some risk of the odium now attached to war movies, old-style. However, stage and academe do not necessarily march in step. The theatre was slow to come to terms with the ironic model of the play. A. C. Sprague's survey of its stage history[6] makes it clear that the traditional reading remained fairly constant, however much the personal idiom of the Henry might change; and Sprague himself regarded the play as without guile: 'Though by no means without shadows, it is on the whole a clear, straightforward history, and certain subtleties of interpretation, as that Henry was tricked by selfish ecclesiastics into

fighting what was in fact a war of pure aggression, seem out of
keeping with its occasion and purpose.'[7] But that was published in
1964, just as the modern wave was breaking over *Henry V*. For today's
stage, I take Richard David's judgement as exemplary: 'That there are
and have always been two sides to *Henry V* is surely obvious, for in it
the pro-war and anti-war feeling are both perfectly explicit, though
their expression is widely and diversely distributed.'[8] 'The problem . . .
is a matter of balance.'[9] Quite: there is no question of a hysterically
adverse view of Henry and his invasion. It is, rather, a matter of
bringing the darker, more sceptical passages into a living relation with
the heroically straightforward. And that has been the concern of
productions in the contemporary era.

I

Any consideration of *Henry V* on the modern stage must begin with
Olivier's film of 1944. As an event in film history, it does not concern
us, and Olivier's audacious experiments in that medium fall outside
our scope. It does, however, take to a very high level of art, and
achieve a permanent expression of, the traditional reading of the play.
It is, moreover, readily available in cinema and television showings,
and has surely attained a dominant grip on the public consciousness.
It would be absurd to pass it by here.

How far is the Olivier film traditional, and how far occasional? It is
usual to point to the circumstances of 1944, and the film is explicitly
dedicated to the commandos and airborne troops of Great Britain –
'the spirit of whose ancestors it has been humbly attempted to
recapture . . .'. The Normandy landings offered a massive analogue to
the plot. As Raymond Durgnat points out, events supply a 'sliding
symbolism', not a consistent code: 'the English are the English but
Agincourt is D-Day where the French are Germans until Henry courts
Katherine, whereupon the French are probably the French'.[10] Of
course the wartime needs governed the central concept – a virile and
likeable leader engaged in a just war. One can, however, over-
emphasize the special needs of 1944. Olivier had played Henry on
stage before in Tyrone Guthrie's production of 1937,[11] and there
appears to have been no great disparity between his stage and film
Henrys. The film version, in its regard for the positive virtues
expressed in the text, is rooted in the English stage tradition. The
treatment of the French, though necessarily designed to display them
as foils to the English, is not lacking in affection, charity and respect.

Thus, the propagandist elements are muted: there is, at bottom, no enemy. Compare this absent sense of *enemy* with Eisenstein's *Alexander Nevsky* – acknowledged as a major source for the battle scenes – in which the Teutonic knights are taken with the utmost seriousness. Geduld is right in remarking that 'Audiences have, time and again enjoyed the film without being aware of its partially propagandist purpose . . . as the events of the Second World War recede from us, the picture has come to seem less overtly chauvinistic than say, *Alexander Nevsky*, less propagandist than *The Birth of a Nation, The Battleship Potemkin, Triumph of the Will* and *The Great Dictator . . .*'.[12] The propaganda is of an extraordinarily subtle and advanced quality, relying like all the best propaganda on positive assertions. The film is simply a toughened, refined and intelligent version of the statement that is always present in the text. In essence, the film exhibits that intuitive opportunism, that feeling for audience and occasion, that guides successful theatre at all times.

The playing-text, now available in published form,[13] is our first concern here. It is heavily cut, much more so than was generally understood at the time. By Geduld's count only 1505 lines were retained out of the 3199 lines in the Pelican text.[14] I cannot do better than quote his summary of the cuts:

> The material removed falls into at least six categories:
> (1) background, including both antecedent action and foreshadowing of events that follow the action of the play; (2) much elaboration of idea, argument and detail; (3) all suggestions that England is endangered by internal conspiracy or that Scotland is a potential threat; (4) much material involving the comic characters; (5) passages and incidents revealing Henry's character unlikely to be attractive to modern audiences; (6) miscellaneous material involving the French, including lines that show the French nobles to be more spirited, worthy adversaries than the rather weak, brash figures they are made to appear in the film.[15]

For details of these cuts, I refer the reader to Geduld's close analysis on pages 48–51. Here I select some of the leading cuts. The episode of the traitors goes, taking with it the suggestion that England is seriously disaffected. Henry's character, though much simplified, gains from the excision of some darker passages. He does not have to condemn Bardolph, nor threaten the citizens of Harfleur with pillage, rape and murder, nor order the execution of the French prisoners. The trait of self-justification is pared away from his lines. Above all, the great soliloquy before Agincourt ends with 'Had the forehand and vantage of a king'; so the cut includes the lines in which Shakespeare's ironic intent is perhaps clearer than anywhere else in the full text:

The slave, a member of the country's peace,
Enjoys it, but in gross brain little wots
What watch the king keeps to maintain the peace,
Whose hours the peasant best advantages.

The broad strokes of the film capture the most positive elements in the surviving text. The Pirandellian opening, taking us to the Globe (backstage, too), presents a genuine community: 'It is a bristling, lively place, democratic in the sense that commoners, gentlemen and nobles watch the same play.'[16] The audience rapport with the players includes an affection for Ely (Robert Helpmann), a silly and ludicrous figure who is Olivier's agent for obscuring the *Realpolitik* of I, i, and I, ii. Canterbury (Felix Aylmer), equally didactic to his stage and Globe audience, loses his scroll in the vast pile of Salic memoranda. Ely hands him the wrong document, receives a slap on the hand and throws the documents in the air. A moment later King and courtiers are scrabbling on the floor. It is a superbly comic expedient, and it completely dissolves the serious intent of the scene. The superciliousness of the French Ambassador and the Dauphin's insolence seem to create their own provocations. There is in context no question that it is right and natural for Henry to teach the French a lesson.

The French, for their part, appear as illustrations from *Les très riches heures du duc de Berri*. The stylized pictorial arrangements and their languid movements and poses identify the spirit of Charles VII's court: it is bored, overcivilized, decadent, a world away from the vitality and passion of the English. It is, moreover, a society dramatically confined to a single stratum, the Court: there is nothing corresponding to the intelligent toughness of the English soldiery and the middle-class professionalism of the Scots, Irish, Welsh and English career officers. The King is a rather endearing dotard, the Dauphin spoilt and vain, the Dukes of Bourbon and Orleans lightweights. The Princess is of course charming, and the Constable a noble and prescient figure; however, the French over all appear far less formidable than the English.

It is necessary not to slant the Anglo-French contest too much, else the worth of the triumph is diminished. The Constable (Leo Genn) is allowed full weight as the Champion of France, who leads the charge and engages Henry in single combat. The French Herald, Montjoy (Ralph Truman), projects a presence superior to the English Herald. Montjoy, exchanging a glance almost of complicity with Henry before Agincourt ('We both have our jobs to do' is the unspoken message), establishes the full equality of France, whatever the limitations of her current leaders. The battle is decided on purely technical grounds: the English, mudstained and indomitable, hold their position against opponents who approach the battle as though it were a tournament. Archery, in combination with improvised defence works, defeats cavalry.

Agincourt is presented by Shakespeare as a dramatically (not technically) inevitable triumph; and Olivier concurred with the arrangements that the most positive areas of the text invite. One leaves the film with a multitude of impressions: the good humour and vitality of the English; the beauty and decadence of the French, whose values are none the less desired by the victors; the vigil before Agincourt, and the most stirring battle-speech in all literature; the unbearably exciting movement of the charge to Walton's finest score; the deep harmonies of the final reconciliation, and the return to the Globe. Nothing has been falsified, and everything in Olivier's film is (I believe) stated or implied in the text. But the secret play, the reservations in that text, have been cut out with a surgical intelligence and precision. And it is the 'other' play that has exercised its fascination over a later generation.

II

The 'other' play took a long time to emerge; and the reasons for delay lay primarily with audiences, for directors must have been aware of the academic reservations about *Henry V*. For a decade after the Olivier film audiences were, in a direct sense, postwar: they looked back to the war, which many had fought in or otherwise experienced, and they took Olivier's as the yardstick against which subsequent productions were measured. It is not necessary to dwell on Richard Burton's Henry at the Old Vic, 1955, under Michael Benthall's direction. Benthall and Burton supplied variations on the traditional pattern, centring on a romantic star casting. Burton brought his own military experience to the part, and his 'How now, what's the matter?' had the genuine ring of the orderly officer's inquiry. Here, as with *Coriolanus*, the military bond between actor and audience was important. The reviewers took it for granted that Burton's interpretation was to be compared with Olivier's.[17] Ten years from the war had apparently changed little.

But change is perpetual if not easily visible. It is clear that the shift in sensibility, which dates itself to around 1956, must have been operating on the assumptions that supported the traditional *Henry V*.

Paradoxically, this emerges from the lack of evidence; for *Henry V* received few revivals in the decade 1955–64. Between the Benthall–Burton version and the RSC's of 1964, the play entered a kind of limbo: too far from the war, not distanced enough for a thoroughgoing re-examination. Trewin lists three productions only for those years,[18] one of them by the National Youth Theatre (1962). Of the other two, Bernard Miles' production at the Mermaid (1960) is remembered, if at all, for its battle-dress, 'the only recorded production in which the second half began with Chorus trying to play "Roses of Picardy" on a mouth organ'.[19] John Neville's Old Vic production of the same year featured a Mother Courage wagon, a desperate expedient that failed to convince critics of the contemporary relevance of the piece, or to reconcile them to its 'crude tub-thumping patriotism'.[20] *Henry V*, it is clear, had already entered upon an era in which it had few friends.

III

One way of getting at the shifts in *Henry V* is to consider two productions at Stratford, Ontario, in 1956 and 1966. Both were directed by Michael Langham, and they offer a sure guide to the times. In 1956 the lead was Christopher Plummer, then a rising young actor of 26, very much the Canadian counterpart of Richard Burton. Brooks Atkinson found him enormously appealing:

> . . . his Henry V is just about ideal. Although the character has drive and courage, he also has a certain boyish modesty that disciplines the braggadocio. He accepts the responsibilities of his office willingly but with underlying humility. He is not showy. The performance is crisp and winning within the framework of an organization of friends and colleagues.[21]

The *Shakespeare Quarterly* reviewer concurred:

> Henry V . . . was allowed to grow as a man and as a king in equal proportions . . . Mr Plummer was able to make Henry V seem a positive saint when confronted by his casuistical bishops, a warrior when compared with the vaunting and empty French nobles, a man of quick temper when he walked amongst his private soldiers, and a humble but ardent lover when he confronted Kate.[22]

The reviews suggest no hint of directorial reservation, based on the clerics' manoeuvres. The most interesting feature of the production was its French-Canadian casting for the French parts, which created a dimension not available outside Canada: 'For Canadians the play also became an extremely vital political tract as the last act slowly worked out a compromise between the beaten French and the victorious English.'[23] The French-Canadian connection aside, this was a well--judged restatement of the traditional reading, centred on a romantic actor of the highest quality.

All that had changed by 1966. For his second essay, Michael Langham offered a new concept. The change of tone was marked, as his programme-notes divulge:

> What has this jingoistic national anthem of a play to do with our age? It glorifies war, exploits the inanities of nationalism, is offensively class-conscious, and – as if to encourage philistine thinking in Canada – is patently and exultantly anti-French. Why then are we performing it? – Just to satisfy those who only think old-world Establishment thoughts?[24]

The defensive note is striking. *Henry V* is now to be justified, not revelled in. The play has become, not exactly ripe for a Director's Index, but something to be treated with the greatest caution. Hence, Langham disclaimed a decisive view of it, preferring to let the audience make its own judgement. He was prepared 'to send people forth from the theatre wondering which view was right, rather than saying (*a*) what a glorious, patriotic play *Henry V* is, or (*b*) what a literal bloody mess war is'.[25] Those who preferred the second alternative were not deprived of guidance from the programme, which included quotations from *Dulce Et Decorum Est*, anti-Henry commentaries from Hazlitt, John Palmer and Harold Goddard, and a picture of Vietnam.

The lead role, formerly Plummer's, was allotted to the very different talent of Douglas Rain, 'an actor whose genius resides largely in his capacity for anonymity, who is without that magnetic stage presence essential to a romantic and epic treatment of *Henry V*. The decision to have a solid, tough and realistic production, not an airy and romantic one was in the circumstances inevitable.'[26] Castings determine productions; but productions determine castings. Langham's choice of Rain was a synthesis of strategic requirements. It followed that the production should emphasize the realistic, gory and brutal aspects of the play, which it did. Much blood flowed during the Agincourt scenes, and the slaughter of the English boys and French prisoners was unsparingly presented. Langham 'spares no feelings to make his point that neither this war, nor by inference any other, is "romantic". When the red nosed clown Bardolph is hanged for stealing, he has him dumped at the king's feet, his throat bloodied by the hangman's rope, dead and foul in death.'[27] The same reviewer found the clowns 'grimy and generally repulsive'. Chorus himself (William Hutt) seemed to have reservations about the war, and a detached, faintly sardonic tone characterized his commentaries.[28] This was no wholehearted restatement of the classic Choric apologia for Henry.

The production grasped the heroic and exemplary elements in the text, but projected them in a changed idiom. This in itself sufficiently distinguished the two armies: 'The English were never under any illusions about war; the romantic view of it was given to some of the French . . . In keeping with the spirit of the production, the French were given more dignity than they sometimes are . . .'.[29] It is characteristic of recent productions, though not exclusive to them, that the French are accorded a full respect.

It is no less a characteristic that *Henry V* is viewed as the extension of *Henry IV*, Parts 1 and 2: hence, the director may concentrate, as did Langham, on the theme of the King's education. This, in a penetrating review, was advanced by John Pettigrew as the key to the production:

Mr Rain's Henry V was the young man learning his job, attentive to the Archbishop and starting at his passing reference to Hugh Capet's usurpation of the crown, worried indeed whether he might 'with right and conscience' lay claim to France, reluctant to do so despite the urging of his peers until ('being incensed, he's flint') provoked by the Dauphin's tennis balls. He has to learn to lead: the line 'Once more unto the breach, once more' was given off-stage (I suspect for the first time in stage history) and the speech given, and most effectively, not as a powerful set piece of rhetoric but as something worked out in the course of its delivery in a desperate effort to get exhausted and beaten troops back into battle. In the Crispin's Day speech we had again a man working terribly hard to find words to encourage despondent men in an apparently hopeless situation, but development was clear: as Henry beckoned his men to hear him, he was confident, now, in his oratorical powers, daring even to act and quaver 'These wounds I had on Crispin's Day' in the voice of an old man. But if confident in his own powers, Henry remained far from confident about the battle (his 'How thou pleasest, God, dispose the day!' was given fatalistically, not ringingly) and all the more fearful about its outcome because Williams' words had stung him to an anger that reflected his uneasy recognition of his moral responsibility for his men. Williams' comments had forced Henry to see how true it is that 'Uneasy lies the head that wears a crown'; no wonder his two soliloquies on the morn of Agincourt packed such a wallop. Only when it was finally and absolutely clear that the miracle had occurred did Mr Rain's Henry finally relax; only then was his education complete.[30]

Henry V, presented with acuity and understanding, was thus transformed. Rescrutinized and recast by Langham, it remained, after all,
a modern play. Pettigrew's summary catches the implications: 'a
thoroughly romantic play with a realistic undercurrent became a
realistic play with a romantic undercurrent'.[31]

Langham's two essays make a particularly instructive pairing. It is
now necessary to return to 1964 and the RSC *Henry V* – the archetypal
modernist production and, of course, influential upon Langham.

IV

The traditional version of *Henry V* stands up better if the play is
detached from the other histories and produced in isolation. It may
then appear as a set of rhetorical affirmations, tenuously connected at
best with its Shakespearean fellows and thus with history itself. The
modern approach is to set *Henry V* within its canonical context, and
this brings two substantial gains. The play appears as a working-out of
the process of history, in which Richard II yields to Bolingbroke, who
bequeaths to his son an insecure inheritance which a foreign war may
help to stabilize. And the play completes the education of Henry and
his progress from Hal to the Warrior King. *Education*, the theme of
this approach, offers wider scope to the actor playing Henry – given
that the casting is retained from *Henry IV* – and a subtle justification
of the man: he is still young, still learning.

The RSC *Henry V* was set into the cycle of history plays. In 1963
the Company had staged *The Wars of the Roses* – *Henry VI* and
Richard III adapted to form three plays. In 1964 *Richard II*, *Henry IV*
Parts 1 and 2 and *Henry V* were added, *The Wars of the Roses* being
retained from the previous season. Thus, in 1964 the RSC presented
(in effect) the two tetralogies, composing the entire history cycle. For
the first time the relationships between the whole and the parts were
visible within a single season. As the programme-note to *Richard II*
stated: 'Behind immense variety, the themes and characters are continuously developed through the cycle. As Orestes was hunted in
Greek drama, so Englishmen fight each other to expunge the curse
pronounced upon Bolingbroke's usurpation of the tragically weak
Richard II.'[32] Peter Hall, who with John Barton and Clifford Williams
directed the cycle, perceived it as an enduring analysis of the political
process, with a timeless application. He expounded his sense of the
histories in his introduction to the published text of *The Wars of the
Roses*:

Over the years I became more and more fascinated by the contortions of politicians, and by the corrupting seductions experienced by anybody who wields power. I began to collect 'sanctions' – those justifications which politicians use in the Press or on television to mask the dictates of their party politics or their personal ambitions . . . I realised that Shakespeare's history plays were full of such sanctions: 'God', 'Fortune', 'The Common Weal', 'Duty', 'St George', 'England', 'France'. What had seemed conventional rhetoric was really, when spoken by Warwick or Richard III, an ironic revelation of the time-honoured practices of politicians. I realised that the mechanism of power had not changed in centuries. We also were in the middle of a blood-soaked century. I was convinced that a presentation of one of the bloodiest and most hypocritical periods in history would teach many lessons about the present.

We therefore had a clear purpose in our task. With our designer, John Bury, we found a strong visual image for the production – a cruel, harsh world of decorated steel, cold and dangerous.[33]

The steel image expresses the concept. One can rephrase it, for instance via Jan Kott's 'Grand Mechanism' of history, the staircase of power: Hall acknowledges his debt to Kott's *Shakespeare Our Contemporary.*[34] Robert Speaight saw the historical plays as 'a sequence of *pièces noires*. They have their moments of *allégresse;* the sun may be setting in Shallow's Orchard, but it still shines. A golden backdrop conveyed the brief, victorious spring of *Henry V*, and the late medieval Renaissance of *Richard II*. For the rest however, the gibbets dangled their corpses on Blackheath, and our last glimpse of Shrewsbury was Worcester hanging from the nearest tree.'[35] The harshness of the political realities conditions the histories, *Henry V* no less than the others.

Peter Hall's production took the events detailed in the text with the utmost seriousness. The prompt-book reveals fairly light, scattered cuts – the slimming rather than the surgical method. The three conspirators have been concentrated into a single one, Cambridge, a move that intensifies Henry's sense of betrayal. The Archbishop keeps every word of his Salic exposition. Interestingly, the last four lines of the Agincourt soliloquy are cut: the same four lines that Olivier dispensed with, ending in 'Whose hours the peasant best advantages'. Since these lines are vital for a determinedly hostile reading of Henry, it is evident that the director has decided to play fair. Henry is not to be canonized, but neither is he to be impeached.

The major casting confirms the inference. Ian Holm's Henry was thoughtful, intelligent, cool, sceptical. Small of stature, he had undoubted presence, but not a romantic charisma. 'The performance took on a quiet and studious authority which did not cease to grow.'[36]

This was the casting concept that Langham, as we have seen, took up. Gareth Lloyd Evans, writing of the 1966 revival set forth the implications:

> Henry V is workmanlike. It appears in his garb; he is, like those retired military men, turned politician, given to wearing the beret of action and the battledress of combat, attired in the rough-hewn and serviceable. It appears, too, in his manner, which is businesslike, particularly in the first scene, in the French capitulation scene, and (with more than a slight suggestion of Olivier) in the wooing scene. These manifestations of honest, down-to-earth purpose have their source, it would seem, in a conception of the play which underemphasizes the ceremonial aura and its position as an English 'epic'. The martial events leading up to and including the battle of Agincourt are presented as bloody, clobbering and unpleasant. There are no traditional heroics in the speeches of the king to his troops. This is a ragged army led by a leader at times almost desperate with fatigue. The heroism, where it exists, is found almost entirely in sheer dogged pugnaciousness. It is the heroism of the First World War trenches, of attrition, of unsung deeds done as a matter of course, and of men following a leader, not because he is a king, but because he is as tired and as stubbornly determined as they are. It is, in short, democratic twentieth-century heroism.[37]

This leader has taken the decision to make war on the firmest grounds available. Canterbury (Charles Kay) speaks with authority on the Salic issue. Henry 'hears everyone else's advice and then very clearly makes up his own mind. And throughout it is he, realizing the full implications, who is the most reluctant to let slip the dogs of war . . .'[38] Other critics confirm this impression. Henry was 'a conscientious monarch, thinking out the morality of each step that he takes'.[39] Another, more extremely, saw him as 'continually racked by doubt and wounded by guilt'.[40] More clearly than anywhere else, this concept of Henry crystallized in 'O God, thine arm *was* there'.

As for Chorus, he was costumed as a Nicholas Hilliard miniature. Eric Porter (later, Ian Richardson) played him full out for Elizabethan rhetoric. John Russell Brown found this a flaw: 'The Chorus was allowed to orate and make flourishes about a quite different play, as if the directors thought that all he said had to be ironically wrong.'[41] But this, surely, is a legitimate directorial ploy. A perceptible disparity between the Chorus' view of the play and the events actually chronicled in the action is one of the effects Shakespeare has built into the text.

This disparity is, in fact, the pointer to the 'secret play'. John Arden, in a letter to the *New Statesman* protesting against Ronald Bryden's unenthusiastic review of the RSC production, phrased it thus:

The *surface* meaning of *Henry V* is certainly that 'Agincourt was a lovely war', and I have no doubt that this was the meaning that Shakespeare intended his audience (and actors) to find in it. But there are so many corrections of this view in the structure of the play that one is forced to wonder if the author had not become prematurely disillusioned with his hero and, while ostensibly following the line laid down by Holinshed, written what is a secret play within the official one.[42]

It is not necessary to agree with Arden's 'prematurely disillusioned' suggestion to accept the tenor of this reading. Arden went on to identify the sequence of clerics' dialogue, the Salic speech, the decision to invade, and the tennis-balls incident: this seemed to him the core of the unofficial version of the campaign. Agincourt might have been heroic, the decision to invade France was not: the 'secret play' is the description, necessarily oblique and elliptical, of the total forces involved in the Agincourt operation.

In all, the RSC *Henry V* of 1964 managed to be pro-Henry – this side of idolatry – anti-war and anti-romantic. The reviewer who found the point of departure 'I think the king is but a man as I am'[43] made, I think, a shrewd estimate. By 1966, when the (somewhat recast) production had matured and public opinion stabilized, it seemed less strange an interpretation. *The Spectator*, summing up the 1966 revival, thought that the RSC *Henry V*, together with the other histories,

> is now generally agreed to have been a vast success; partly, no doubt, because generations of reverential treatment have bred a definite truculence towards Shakespeare, or towards the notions – nobility of war, pluckiness of the soldiery, excellence of the heroic virtues – which he is said to have put about. So an anti-romantic production, which turns Henry V into one of the lads and has him deliver his Crispin Crispian speech in stony silence, without even the faintest breath of cheer from the troops, found the ground to some extent prepared for it.[44]

V

And so to the *Henry V* produced for the centenary season at the Royal Shakespeare Theatre in 1975, directed by Terry Hands and with Alan Howard as Henry. Widely celebrated, this production continued the line of development inaugurated by the RSC in 1964 and Stratford, Ontario, in 1966. The 1975 season presented *Henry V* in repertory with the two parts of *Henry IV*; hence, the education of the King remained, as before, the theme. Hands' strategy, as in the productions of a decade earlier, was to hold the balance: 'he is not going to heroise

Hal and glamorize conquest, nor does he want to slant things the other way, satirising and condemning a bloodthirsty crusade'.[45] As Irving Wardle saw it,

> *Henry V* is a notoriously difficult piece to square with the postwar conscience, and for some people it is acceptable only as a nationalist propaganda pageant with a private and sceptical play going on inside. That is not the treatment it gets in this version in which Operation Agincourt is still allowed to emerge as heroic; but the tone is none the less as queasy as anyone could wish.[46]

This 'queasy' tone was a logical result of Hands' analysis, which in turn was based on the historical moment of the revival:

> In 1945 Laurence Olivier's film had served to stimulate the nation as a whole. The problems of that time were specifically national so the 'patriotic' element in the play was specifically emphasised. From the character of Henry himself all doubt and uncertainty were removed. And so largely the play has been interpreted ever since. However the non-specific unity of 1945, that of armies, is less important to us than the specific unity explored in the play itself: that of individuals aware of their responsibilities, both to themselves and to each other, voluntarily accepting some abdication of that individuality in a final non-hierarchic interdependence – a real brotherhood.[47]

The last clause sounds oddly reminiscent of an argument in favour of an incomes policy or a voluntary pay code – matters much on the national mind in 1975. Hands is correct in characterizing the play as 'full of doubt. Full of uncertainty . . .'[48] They were hardly the qualities for which the text had been celebrated in the past, and the director was presumably responding to a changed perception of national situation as much as to a changed perception of the play.

Farrah, the designer, felt that

> what we wanted to create was not a box of illusions, but something that freed the audience's imaginations and made them conjure their own illusions. And, because we were beginning the play as if the actors were rehearsing, we wanted an area that was clearly defined, but which also could be seen to be an organic part of the building . . . So we stripped the stage; we cleared it of everything extraneous, to make it as austere and as bare as possible . . . we built a new stage-platform with a one-in-twelve rake. It was a stage designed to launch the actors into the audience.[49]

The actors sauntered, in fact, rather than launched themselves into the opening. The audience discovered them in workshop gear, jogging, improvising, lying down, studying. One of the actors

detached himself from the others, and came forward: 'Oh for a Muse
of fire . . .' And Chorus (Emrys James) indicated, as he spoke, the
'flat unraisèd spirits' lying around the stage. The drab, modern garb –
inviting a detached and sceptical response – was retained into the
clerics' scene, and the Council. Thereafter the action reverted to
period costume. This was especially gorgeous for the French, as is
usual; but Hands has an interesting comment here: 'Theatrically,
period costume is an outmoded convention. Used here it helps to
accentuate the fact that the French are frozen in an era that has
already passed.'[50] The French, all in golden armour, were fifteenth-
century; the English, in greys and brown, appeared in a timeless
ambience suggestive of world war combat. For the 'Breach' scene, a
wall rose from the floor – steeply raked, dangerous – and from it
Henry delivered his perilously thrilling speech. Throughout, the
English scenes emphasized the realities and human costs of war, while
the French still inhabited a beautifully illuminated Book of Hours.

For Alan Howard, Henry's experience is a voyage towards self-
discovery; and this is the most important reason in his decision to
make war.[51] The most searching examination of Henry's identity
occurs in the night scene before Agincourt. He is still masking
himself, assuming the role of army commander.[52]

> Then Williams confronts him with the whole question of the king's
> responsibility for his soldiers in war. I think he answers Williams somewhat
> inadequately, except that he does say 'every subject's soul is his own', which
> is a sudden and extraordinary admission of personal responsibility, his first
> articulation of that idea. He says that he *embraces* Williams' challenge, not
> that he accepts it, or some other weaker term. And I think he means that:
> he welcomes all the implications of that challenge, including the fact that it
> is *his* own challenge, turned upon himself.'[53]

(Since the speech is cut after 'every subject's soul is his own', the
playing-text makes it the major point of Henry's response.) Thus, all
is set for the great discovery of personal and communal identity that is
the core of the Agincourt experience:

> The Crispin's day speech finally unites the English. No longer are they
> linked merely by such external things as birth, status or nationality; their
> unity and determination have become 'interior', a state of mind, and
> perhaps heart: 'All things are ready if our minds be so'.[54]

The RSC production rested on the personality and capacities of its
Henry. On the one hand, Alan Howard demonstrated the traditional

qualities that the part calls for – a commanding stage presence, good looks, a voice that has to deliver the battlefield goods, all to be checked against a standard marked 'Olivier'; on the other hand, he displayed a moral awareness of the drama, a continually surprising inventiveness, and an intelligence directed always towards exploring the self-doubt and pain in the role. Irving Wardle details some of these moments:

> Howard grapples on the floor with the treacherous Scroop, as a father who has let him down. He practically vomits after hurling the barbarous threats at Harfleur; and again half way through reading the roll call of the French dead. His stainless adventure is haunted by the Eastcheap ghosts; and when Bardolph is caught robbing the church Howard has to stand and give the execution order with Pistol looking him straight in the eye; an ordeal that shakes his nerve with the French herald. Then, in a wonderful transition, he begins a halting speech, hits by accident on a joke and a smile of surprised delight steals across his face at his own powers of recovery, and his capacity to keep on acting.[55]

All the best reviews, in fact, revert in some form to this sense of moral queasiness which now, one may hazard, is the central experience of *Henry V* for today's audience. Benedict Nightingale describes well the impact of this Henry, and of his war:

> Mr Howard is all imagination and self-awareness . . . Ghosts haunt his queasy mind, principal among them his own father, usurper of Richard II's throne – witness the hoarse panic of Mr Howard's prayer that this crime should be remembered 'not today, O Lord, O, not today'. As this suggests, he's a pretty scrupulous sort, always uncomfortable about the responsibilities thrust upon him. 'May I with right and conscience make this claim?' he asks of the invasion of France, his earnest self-doubt quaintly contrasting with the Archbishop's complacent bleating. The production leaves us free to conclude that his military adventure was a moral outrage; but it doesn't give us any reason to suppose that it was lightly or cynically perpetrated by him.[56]

And that, effectively, seems to be where *Henry V* has for the present come to rest. The continuing success of the 1975 RSC production (which was still being re-staged in 1978) testifies to its appeal to the contemporary mind. *Henry V* can no longer be experienced as a simple paean; the evidence, in and out of the text, forbids it. Neither can it be dismissed as if it were an object against which to mount a demonstration. In opting for personal and communal identity, Terry Hands chose the theme that avoids excesses of response. The strategy, for today, is well advised, and the director thus managed 'to square anti-militarist scruples with a full-blooded treatment of the great national folk tale'.[57] On those terms, the play remains. What happens to that text in future will no doubt be determined less by directors than by history.

NOTES

1 William Hazlitt, *Characters of Shakespeare's Plays and Lectures on the English Poets* (London: Macmillan, 1903), p. 127.

2 Edwin Wilson (ed.) *Shaw on Shakespeare* (New York: Dutton, 1961), pp. 101–2.

3 See Paul A. Jorgensen, 'Accidental judgements, casual slaughters, and purposes mistook: critical reactions to Shakespeare's *Henry the Fifth*', in *Shakespeare Association Bulletin*, vol. XXII (1947), pp. 51–61.

4 Gerald Gould, 'A new reading of *Henry V*', *English Review* (1919). Reprinted in *Shakespeare: Henry V*, ed. Michael Quinn, Casebook series (London: Macmillan, 1969), pp. 81–94.

5 For example, John Palmer, *Political Characters of Shakespeare* (London: Macmillan, 1945), pp. 180–249; Harold C. Goddard, *The Meaning of Shakespeare*, 2 vols (Chicago, Ill.: University of Chicago Press, 1951), Vol. I, pp. 215–68; Roy Battenhouse, '*Henry V* as heroic comedy', in *Essays on Shakespeare and Elizabethan Drama*, ed. Richard Hosley (Columbia, Miss.: University of Missouri Press, 1962), pp. 163–82.

6 A. C. Sprague, *Shakespeare's Histories: Plays for the Stage* (London: Society for Theatre Research, 1964).

7 Ibid., p. 92.

8 Richard David, 'Of an age and for all time: Shakespeare at Stratford', *Shakespeare Survey 25* (1972), p. 168.

9 Ibid.

10 Raymond Durgnat, *Films and Feelings* (Cambridge, Mass.: MIT Press, 1967), p. 262.

11 Where, perhaps, he gleaned the idea of playing the clerics' scenes for laughs. Laurence Kitchin discusses his delivery of 'May I with right and conscience make this claim?' in *Mid-Century Drama* (London: Faber, 1960), pp. 50–1.

12 Harry M. Geduld, *Filmguide to 'Henry V'* (Bloomington, Ind: Indiana University Press, 1973), p. 66.

13 In *Film Scripts One*, ed. George P. Garrett, O. B. Hardison, Jnr, and Jane R. Gelfman (New York: Appleton-Century-Crofts, 1971).

14 Geduld, op. cit., p. 48.

15 Ibid.

16 Jack J. Jorgens, *Shakespeare on Film* (Bloomington, Ind., and London: Indiana University Press, 1977), p. 123.

17 Kenneth Tynan found him 'a cunning warrior, stocky and astute, unafraid of harshness or of curling the royal lip. The gallery gets no smiles from him, and the soldiery none but the scantest commiseration. Though it sometimes prefers rant to exuberance, this is an honest performance, true and watchful and ruthless' (*A View of the English Stage* (Frogmore, St Albans: Paladin, 1976), p. 164).

18 J. C. Trewin, in *Shakespeare on the English Stage 1900–1964* (London: Barrie & Rockliff, 1964) offers three appendixes: for productions in the West End, at the Old Vic, and at Stratford-upon-Avon.

19 Ibid., p. 231.

20 Peter Roberts, *Plays and Players* (July 1960), p. 11.

21 *The New York Times*, 19 June 1956.
22 Arnold Edinborough, 'Consolidation in Stratford, Ontario,' *Shakespeare Quarterly*, vol. VII (1956), p. 405.
23 Ibid., p. 404.
24 Quoted by Arnold Edinborough, 'The Canadian Shakespeare Festival', *Shakespeare Quarterly*, vol. XVII (1966), p. 40.
25 Ibid., p. 401.
26 John Pettigrew, 'Stratford's Festival Theatre: 1966', *Queen's Quarterly*, vol. LXXIII (1966), p. 391.
27 Elliot Norton, *Record American*, 8 June 1966.
28 'Throughout the play he explains those vaulting odes to imagination like a finger-wagging schoolmaster' (Brooks Atkinson, *The New York Times*, 4 June 1966).
29 Pettigrew, op. cit., p. 395.
30 Ibid., p. 396.
31 Ibid., p. 393.
32 *Richard II*, RSC programme-note, 1964.
33 John Barton in collaboration with Peter Hall, *The Wars of the Roses* (London: British Broadcasting Corporation, 1970), pp. x–xi.
34 Ibid., p. xi.
35 Robert Speaight, 'Shakespeare in Britain', *Shakespeare Quarterly*, vol. XV (1964), p. 388.
36 Ibid., p. 386.
37 Gareth Lloyd Evans, 'Shakespeare, the twentieth century and "behaviourism" ', *Shakespeare Survey 20* (1967), p. 139.
38 Bamber Gascoigne, *The Observer*, 7 June 1964.
39 Milton Shulman, *Evening Standard*, 28 May 1965.
40 Alan Brien, *Sunday Telegraph*, 7 June 1964.
41 John Russell Brown, 'Three kinds of Shakespeare', *Shakespeare Survey 18* (1965), p. 151.
42 John Arden, letter to *New Statesman*, 19 June 1964.
43 David Pryce-Jones, *The Spectator*, 12 June 1964.
44 Hilary Spurling, *The Spectator*, 19 August 1966.
45 Benedict Nightingale, *New Statesman*, 18 April 1975.
46 Irving Wardle, *The Times*, 22 January 1976.
47 Sally Beauman (ed.), *The Royal Shakespeare Company Centenary Production of 'Henry V'* (Oxford: Pergamon, 1976), p. 15.
48 Ibid., p. 15.
49 Ibid., p. 31.
50 Ibid., p. 137.
51 Howard enumerates the other reasons in his analysis of the role: ibid., pp. 54–5. Concerning the force of the Salic speech, Hands offers an analysis of the cuts that were tried (8½ lines, beginning 'Nor did the French possess the Salic land'):

> These lines were cut at a very late stage – and perhaps should not have been.
>
> The speech itself is difficult. Erudite, involved, historically inaccurate, it may be intended as a political ploy with a comic denouement. In which case boring your audience is a valid technique.
>
> On the other hand, it may be a real attempt by the Archbishop to explain the problems of succession.

If it is the former, pace is acceptable and these lines could be included. We focus then upon the technique of the speaker. If it is the latter, the speech becomes interminable. The lines should go.

I confess that Derek Smith (Canterbury) and I never quite made up our minds between the two methods.

Having watched the play for eight months I now feel more drawn to the former interpretation. The lines could go back. [Ibid., p. 110.]

52 Howard discusses Henry's role-playing propensities: ibid., pp. 53–4.
53 Ibid., p. 58.
54 Ibid., p. 193.
55 Wardle, op. cit.
56 Nightingale, op. cit.
57 Irving Wardle, *The Times*, 13 July 1977.

CHAPTER FIVE

Hamlet

No demonstration is required that *Hamlet* is uniquely responsive to the *Zeitgeist*. This applies to all people – 'I have a smack of Hamlet about me, if I may say so,' said Coleridge – and all peoples: 'There is something especially Japanese about Hamlet,' a recent Japanese critic has said. The play easily takes on a national tang. A leading Polish director once observed to me: '*Hamlet* is always successful with us. Hamlet is always a Pole, and Fortinbras is the Soviet army.' *Hamlet* has always enjoyed a special esteem, popular and cult, since its earliest days – the time when the discerning Gabriel Harvey was noting in his marginalia that *Hamlet* and *Lucrece* 'have it in them to please the wiser sort'. It has never (in western Europe and North America, at least) been long out of favour, though it is true that a straight version has sometimes had to be discovered – as in France, where a reasonably unadapted text was not played until late in the nineteenth century. The play continues to be revived at regular and frequent intervals, and it will not usually be possible to detect a radical discontinuity between one revival and the next. *Hamlet* is organically and effortlessly absorbed into the life of its times, not lending itself to surprising rediscoveries; though naturally individual Hamlets have made the part resonate with great effect. It is necessary, then, to approach *Hamlet* with a broad time-span in mind; otherwise the details of the individual productions will tend to lose their significance. I want first to sketch in some general considerations that apply to *Hamlet*, in England, since 1945.

I

Hamlet is uniquely concentrated upon its leading actor. The physical presence of Hamlet is in great measure the play. And ideas of beauty, which include male good-looks, change. For most of this century,

Hamlets have been classically good-looking: Scofield, Gielgud, Forbes-Robertson, to name a few. Sometimes they appear, in their faded photographs, delicate, romantic, Byronic to a fault – they rise up as a collective cliché. For this is not the admired style of looks today. The type of face which used to be described as 'matinée idol' – Greek profile, regular features, smooth black/blond hair – is seldom seen, or is used for special effects (Edward Fox, say). In its place a more irregular, perhaps more individual and vital, countenance is favoured. This happens to apply to actresses, too, but our concern is with leading actors. And, of course, the preference for a different style is not morally neutral, socially null. It is not a matter of technical fashion, of raising or lowering a hem a few inches. It is an affair of the greatest social significance, involving an entire value-system. By the 1960s, as Elsom notes, 'suave actors had been replaced by rough ones as heroes, metropolitan accents by regional ones, complacent young men by angry ones, stylish decadents by frustrated, "working-class", anti-heroes'.[1] And *Hamlet* could only follow the times. The 'classical' Hamlets sought to realize the implications of *noble, nobility;* the Hamlets of the 1960s turned towards the 'plebeian'. (I use the antithesis as an approximation of style. Kenneth Tynan divides all actors into poets and peasants.) And this orientation responds to a deep chord in the text, for a virile, individual, resentful Hamlet at odds with the Establishment physicalizes the concept that 'noble' is a genteelism. We saw plainly the conflict between the noble and plebeian views of Hamlet with Peter Hall's striking production of 1965–6, with David Warner in the lead. It is true that one distinguished critic saw in him 'an Etonian',[2] but this is a subtlety of role-playing and interpretation; for the general public and critics, this was the least noble and most demotic Hamlet they ever saw. There has been a reaction since (no one could think of Alan Howard's presence as other than aristocratic), but the controversy marks a deep shift in our times. This was also apparent in Nicol Williamson's Hamlet (on stage and on film), who suggested a snarling Tyneside student, in revolt at least in part against the genteel Southern Establishment. And the Hamlet of 1976 (Albert Finney) was certainly a raw, vital presence, 'provincial' in the positive sense. These matters are delicate, and depend at any one time on the persona of the actor available for the part. But that may be a way of saying that the director has to acquiesce in the pre-selections of the system itself, and choose from his available range a Hamlet who appeals to, as he embodies, the new constellation of values. Over all, it must be true that our ideas of Hamlet are modified by, and with, our changing tastes in male looks and manner; and these are associated with social and perhaps political values.

Another profound change lies in the age of Hamlets. Unlike policemen, Hamlets not only seem younger, they are younger. Forbes-Robertson played his last Hamlet in his sixty-fourth year. That, of course, is impossible today. It is not so striking that Olivier was in his fortieth year when he filmed *Hamlet*, for that is the age at which Albert Finney, in 1976, played Hamlet at the National Theatre. But one can hazard that 40 is now the upper limit for an actor to play Hamlet, and that tastes run to a much younger player. This in itself marks a very broad band of change: Gielgud remarks (in the context of *Much Ado about Nothing*), 'But, as was the fashion until the advent of the cinema, the leading characters in Shakespeare were played by actors who were really far too old, and the rest of the cast had to be balanced accordingly'.[3] No doubt there are technical reasons connected with the cinema for this change; celluloid (as in Kozintsev's Russian film) can too cruelly reveal a Hamlet who is scarcely young enough to be Gertrude's son. But the main reason is probably a change of orientation that in the West has for a generation emphasized youth and, moreover, defines youth as under 30. The importance of the *young* audience means that this perspective is bound to tell on the production. The *éclat* of David Warner's Hamlet sprang from the fact that he looked like, and was, a contemporary of a heavy proportion of the audience.

And this perception – essentially, the 'young' perception – not only accounts for the taste in young Hamlets, but also governs the perception of the total play (regardless of the age of the lead) that has gained ground. All productions have to balance the individual-versus-society statement contained in the text. The later productions, certainly of the mid and late 1960s, emphasized an adverse view of the Danish court. This is projected partly as a perception of Hamlet's own mind, partly as a contemporary view of society as restrictive, bureaucratic, illiberal and threatening. It is best summed up, perhaps, in a moment of David Warner's Hamlet that John Russell Brown has caught: 'When pursued by Rosencrantz and Guildenstern and the officers, his "Here *they* come" is illuminated with a contemporary inflection that marks "they" as a composite description of restrictive and uncomprehending authority; the speech is far more important than the simple identification that it seems to be on the printed page.'[4] Who would have thought the third-person plural pronoun so powerful an image? Yet it clearly crystallizes a perception of the action. The same concept emerges from the photographs of Hamlet in his opening scene, seated at the Council table and flanked by, hemmed in by, Polonius and Claudius – not, as traditionally, isolated at the other end of the stage. It is a long way from the Elsinore of Stratford, 1948, where the isolation of Hamlet was projected against a reasonable, if Victorianly conventional, court (itself, perhaps, a reflection of G. Wilson Knight's famous essay in *The Wheel of Fire*, where Hamlet is viewed as a negative and destructive force in his society).

And, finally, another way of looking at *Hamlet* on the modern stage is to take into account perhaps the finest piece of *Hamlet* criticism in the era: Tom Stoppard's *Rosencrantz and Guildenstern Are Dead* (1966). Formally, this is a play constructed on those fragments of *Hamlet* that contain speeches by Rosencrantz and Guildenstern. Effectively, it is the most notable contribution in contemporary English drama (saving Pinter) to the theatre of the absurd. Hamlet's problem, of making sense out of his universe, is bequeathed downwards to his friends; together they constitute an anti-hero, a dual image of two uncomprehending and unlucky lads who find their assignment beyond their powers. It happens that *Rosencrantz and Guildenstern Are Dead* was enormously popular for several years, and is still played (and studied) with a frequency that suggests it has entered into the permanent repertory, and thus the modern consciousness. May it not be possible that, for an increasing number of people, *Hamlet* is the other half of *Rosencrantz and Guildenstern Are Dead*?

II

I turn now from these general considerations to a study of some major stagings of *Hamlet*. The first is Michael Benthall's production at Stratford (1948) with the lead alternating between Paul Scofield and Robert Helpmann. The play-text as revealed in the prompt-book would today be considered odd and old-fashioned. It is understood, naturally, that heavy cuts are virtually inevitable because of the inordinate length of a conflation of Second Quarto and Folio (the exceptional instances when the full text is played, such as at the National Theatre, 1976, are always celebrated on that account), and that, moreover, the primary questions of cutting concern Hamlet's part. In detail: the opening scene loses the 'armaments race' dialogue (I, i, 70–111). In scene two, Cornelius and Voltimand disappear (from a large cast, one presumably not too troubled by questions of expense). Hamlet in his first speech loses the four lines beginning 'Nor windy suspiration', but his soliloquy is uncut. Reynaldo

Changing Styles in Shakespeare

disappears, and with him the Polonius–Reynaldo scene (II, i). Otherwise, there are light cuts only until II, ii, where thirty lines of dialogue about child actors go (very reasonably, all but scholars will feel). 'O what a rogue and peasant slave' loses only the traditional 'Plucks off my beard' – a clean-shaven Hamlet is apparently a total necessity of theatre. 'To be or not to be' is uncut. However, a third of the advice to the Players goes (III, ii) and the dumb show is eliminated. Much of the play scene disappears, but 'Our wills and fates do so contrary run . . . their ends none of their own' stays. So far the cuts are not especially controversial; now they assume a direction. At the end of the closet scene with Gertrude, and following 'but Heaven hath pleased it so', the text loses 'To punish me with this, and this with me,/That I must be their scourge and minister' (III, iv, 174–5). This piece of self-exculpation is necessary to an adverse view of Hamlet, as also to an especially helpless and impotent Hamlet. Also cut is 'I'll lug the guts into the neighbour room' (line 212), always the sign of a sensitive and not overly masculine Hamlet. (John Neville cut it from his 1957 performance.) In the same vein, Hamlet in his confrontation with Claudius (IV, iii) loses the 'Your worm is your only emperor for diet . . . guts of a beggar' passage (lines 22–33). Earthiness is being dispatched. So also goes the speculation on Alexander's dust (V, i). But the major excision is in V, ii. The first fifty-five lines disappear, the scene now beginning 'So Rosencrantz and Guildenstern go to it', and ' 'Tis dangerous when the baser nature' down to 'And a man's life's no more than to say "One" ' is also cut (lines 60–74). This ancient stratagem of the theatre is today intolerable; it deprives us of the only late occasion when Hamlet is discussing his *case* with his friend: his recent past, the bill of indictment against Claudius, his motives, the way he sees himself. The cut passage also contains the astounding admission that he *hoped* to be King ('Popped in between th' election and my hopes') which ought to cast a shaft of brilliant light on the recesses of Hamlet's mind.

Again, the final passages are somewhat simplified. After Hamlet's first two lines of asking pardon of Laertes, the cut extends from 'And you must needs have heard' through Laertes' part-refusal to 'But till that time . . .' (V, ii, 239–61). Thus Hamlet's psychologically interesting repudiation of his 'sore distraction' goes, as does Laertes' temporizing. The final Hamlet dialogue is uncut, but the English Ambassadors disappear. The cut runs from 'The sight is dismal' to Horatio's 'Are here arrived' (lines 378–88), and from Fortinbras' 'Let us haste to hear it' to Horatio's 'On plots and errors happen' (lines 397–406). It is interesting that the passages Stoppard used so effectively at the end of *Rosencrantz and Guildenstern Are Dead* largely disappear here; a different order of effect is sought, simpler, more generalized, less ironic.

It is reasonable now for us to think of it as 'Scofield's' Hamlet, as much the more eminent of the two actors. In fact, the reviews divided praise for Helpmann and Scofield, the former being already a distinguished ballet-dancer. This aspect was taken up by the *New Statesman* reviewer: 'The influence of the ballet is everywhere apparent; and what could be more healthy and fruitful? In the production one may trace to the ballet, I suspect, not only the richness and the colour and the inventiveness of the patterns but also the firm line with which the outline of the action is drawn . . . Mr Benthall is freely called a visual producer. . . .'[5] Thus, the balletic skills of Helpmann (the senior Hamlet) were deployed in a spectacle of rich texture, visual and kinetic. The *mise-en-scène* was Victorian; the set (James Baily) sumptuous and a little distracting. One notes in the prompt-book four footmen (plus two councillors, three ladies, and a page) with occasional business like '*Rosencrantz and Guildenstern take off their hats and coats – footmen take them*'. The stage society is seen as convention-bound and repressive rather than actively inimical to Hamlet. So no decisive concept occurs: it is simply a backcloth against which individual feats of acting are projected. We come back, then, to the Hamlet that the text permits, and it is no surprise to find the *Spectator* critic remarking (on the cutting of 'I'll lug the guts'): 'The sensitive, aesthetic side was emphasized rather than the bitter and astringent. . . . It was easier to believe in Hamlet's love for his mother and Horatio than for his father.' Scofield, additionally, looked like 'a sensitive adolescent who had lost his way'.[6] The main judgement is now clear. This was essentially a prewar *Hamlet*, staged with brio and distinction: it was clearly descended from Gielgud's, the most celebrated Hamlet of his generation. Gielgud had played his last Hamlet only four years earlier, in 1944, a performance which J. C. Trewin found 'his most fluent, his most eloquent (and his bitterest) Hamlet'.[7] Following this tradition, Scofield and Helpmann displayed a poetic and sensitive temperament, one fixed on their mothers. (Cf. the prewar interest in Ernest Jones' theories of an Oedipal Hamlet.) The limitations of the prompt-text scarcely permitted a tougher-minded approach to the part.

III

Michael Redgrave's Hamlet at Stratford (1958), directed by Glen Byam Shaw, is an opportunity to observe the progress of the play after a decade. It is also interesting in that the lead actor was 50. One cannot imagine this occurring today, and it caused a little comment then. The prompt-text shows a subtle and coherent system of cuts, which strike the corpus of the play at a different angle of incidence from Scofield–Helpmann's. The opening scene dispenses with a section of the arms-race and Fortinbras material (I, i, 70–125, 149–57). More surprisingly, Marcellus loses the four golden lines ending 'So hallowed and so gracious is the time', and one immediately wonders if the intention is to cut down the moments of pure poetry. (Here, perhaps, is already the reaction against what Peter Hall used later to call 'the Shakespeare music'.) In scene two Cornelius and Voltimand stay, but Claudius loses half of ' 'Tis sweet and commendable'; rhetoric, like poetry, is to be reduced. Thereafter the cuts are light and reasonable, and the Polonius–Reynaldo scene stays – always a cause of rejoicing to *Hamlet* collectors. The reference to Hamlet's stockings 'down gyvèd to his ankles' goes (it does not suit his appearance in this revival), but the play is left intact hereabouts. The play scene suffers few cuts, and the references to the 'eyrie of children' remain. So does the whole of the 'rugged Pyrrhus' speech, and most of the First Player's reply in the same vein. 'O what a rogue and peasant slave' is uncut, as is 'To be or not to be'. So is Hamlet's advice to the players (III, ii). But now the cuts assume a real direction: four lines of Hamlet–Ophelia dialogue before the play scene go (118–21), including 'That's a fair thought to lie between maids' legs'. The speculation that the sexual element is being toned down for this Hamlet is confirmed by the departure of lines 245–50, which include Hamlet's 'It would cost you a groaning to take off mine edge'. Taken in conjunction with the known presence of Redgrave, this is unmistakably a sign of an intellectual, rational rather than poetical hero. Hamlet is most certainly an *actor*, and the very full retention of the dialogue with the players asserts this; so, implicitly, does the presence of the dumb show; and the 'fellowship in a cry of players' passage stays, to close up the concept.

A little curiously, the 2½ lines of additional speculation in the 'Now might I do it pat' soliloquy are cut (beginning 'And how his audit stands'), perhaps because the director wished to get this speech over rather rapidly and impulsively. (It was whispered.) The main line of the cuts is discernible again in the closet-scene with Gertrude. The elaboration 'Oh, such a deed . . . is thought-sick at the act' (III, iv, 45–51) goes, evidently a rejection of 'poetic' attitudinizing. There is necessarily a strongly sexual element in Hamlet's admonitions to Gertrude, but it is greatly reduced through the long cut 'Sense sure you have . . .' to 'And reason panders will' (III, iv, 71–8), which includes 'You cannot call it love, for at your age/The heyday in the blood is tame. . . .' (It is possible that the director felt that such advice, coming from a 50-year-old, might excite the groundlings' mirth.) There are additional cuts in this dialogue, which help to retain the drive and momentum of the scene, and Hamlet's final speech almost disappears (lines 202–10, 212–13 are cut). 'I'll lug the guts into the neighbour room' once more vanishes, thus demonstrating a Hamlet of refinement and good taste for whom this rough line exhibits an unwelcome dimension of the role. It is surprising how many of Hamlet's lines seem unwelcome to the actor who must speak them; perhaps that is a comment on the psychology of the part. At all events, the text here shows an intellectual–sensitive and not a poetical–sensory Hamlet.

As expected, 'How all occasions' remains uncut. In IV, vii, the second and third speeches disappear: so Claudius does not refer to his reasons, the Queen's love for Hamlet and the public regard for him. Certainly the second reason is information not distinctly available elsewhere, and thus a genuine dimension of the play (Hamlet's political standing) is weakened. Light cuts follow thereafter, but V, ii, suffers no butchery this time. On this, Muriel St Clare Byrne wrote exultantly·

> The text was cut, but kept the Ambassadors and Reynaldo, and above all delighted me by restoring nearly all of 11. 1–74 in V. ii, in which Hamlet describes his foiling of the King's plot against his life – that destructive but traditional cut which has some three centuries of theatre practice behind it, although the importance of the lines, for the full realization of Hamlet's character, is fundamental. Actor and audience alike are trading on their knowledge of this passage if the one presents and the other accepts the Hamlet of the end of the play as the 'changed man', the integrated personality, the complete Prince.[8]

'Nearly all' is an exaggeration. The scene opens with 'Sir, in my heart there was a kind of fighting' (line 4), and thereafter the Hamlet–Horatio exchanges are maintained in skeletal form. There are important losses: 'their defeat/Does by their own insinuation grow . . . mighty opposites' goes, as does the 'is't not to be damned' speculation (lines 68–70): this Hamlet is less concerned with damnation than others. But the bill of indictment against Claudius survives, as does 'And a man's life's no more than to say "One" '. Hamlet's apology to Laertes is cut heavily, from 'What I have done' to 'His madness is poor Hamlet's enemy': this is pre-eminently a sane Hamlet. He loses no more lines, though, and the rest of the play is wound up rapidly. The English Ambassador's speech disappears, and nearly all of Horatio's 'carnal, bloody, and unnatural acts', leaving only 'give order . . . How these things came about'. Horatio's epitome is thus withheld, and he loses also the last three lines of the part. Fortinbras commands the final passages, uncut.

The critics, on the whole, took well to Redgrave's Hamlet, though the overall production (conventional Renaissance costumes) was not highly regarded. It was thoroughly grasped that the determinant of the role was Redgrave's age and authority.

A certain maturity is in any case imposed on him by the actual physical facts. . . . This is a Hamlet of thirty, not a man of action, but not an irresolute either. A reflective young man thrown into the unaccustomed position of having to act, and taking it calmly and reflectively stage by stage. Bitter, but not neurotic, about his mother's marriage, he has experienced no hint of foreknowledge that it needed a murder to bring it off. The ghost's pronouncement does not, as often, come as the confirmation of some deliberately buried fear. It comes – production and acting make it clear – as a complete surprise, a totally new idea to him, difficult to believe, harder to accept. But it must be considered by him as a hypothesis to be tested; step by step he will set out to prove it or disprove it.[9]

The madness, too, as another reviewer saw it, finds an acceptable mode of acting: 'Mr Redgrave's madness is more Pirandello than Shakespeare's – like Pirandello's mock Henry the Fourth, he ranges the lonely corridors quizzing and upbraiding and flattering the hired hands unconvincingly tarted up as Renaissance noblemen, the one living person in a world of make-believe.'[10] All this is cool, logical, convincing; and the critics unite in praising Redgrave's complete intellectual grasp of the part. But it entails a necessary criticism, put well by T.C. Worsley: 'Whatever facet of the Hamlet myth different ages, or different actors, may choose to emphasize, there is one constant – immaturity.'[11] Precisely: the excellence of the actor playing Hamlet so often subjugates a vital facet of the role. (The same order of criticism, justly, was urged against Olivier in his film: that, above all, he was too masculine and decisive.) Curiously, the criticism of the actor seems to parallel the criticism of the text Hamlet: here is someone, greatly gifted, who has yet a fatal flaw, 'one defect'. One settles, then, for the positive qualities that each actor brings. Or, more extreme, one regards the problems from Jonathan Miller's perspective: 'I think of Hamlet as a series of lines to which an infinite series of claimants arrives and competes for. I sometimes think of the Tichborne Claimant. Hamlet is someone who might be someone, were there someone to claim him, and I think the job of rehearsal is to create a circumstance in which claimants will present themselves for examination.'[12] Redgrave settled for authority and intellectual capacity. These qualities proved exceptionally rewarding to many. Muriel St Clare Byrne put him in the Gielgud class: 'I came away feeling I had never encountered either in acting or in criticism a more comprehensive understanding of the text. The quicksilver mind of the man finds its true complement in the mind of the actor, which contradicts throughout, by its unabated liveliness, the "settled melancholy" concept. The vitality and immediacy of his mental reactions give us a more continuously positive awareness of Hamlet himself, the underlying personality, the whole man.'[13] She cites, in discussing the extent to which he revivified the text, this: 'One example of this electric impact with which he charged words and passions throughout the text occurred when Hamlet tells Ophelia he is "very proud, revengeful, ambitious". I have never before realized with a shock, Yes! you could be, and you know these traits in yourself, and do not want your action of justice to be tainted by them.'[14] Good criticism: but this, as we have seen, is an opportunity that rises naturally from the text played. If one is going to make anything of 'ambition', as a real factor, one has to leave in not only Rosencrantz's speculation, 'Why then your ambition makes it one' (II, ii), but also the important dialogue at the beginning of V, ii, most especially 'Popped in between th' election and my hopes'.

Redgrave's Hamlet, in sum, was mature, authoritative, intelligent; a little more astringent than Scofield's, it lacked a certain romantic, poetic and, indeed, sexual dimension. The cuts establish this clearly, even without the criticism. If one takes Scofield as the inheritor of the Gielgud tradition, one can suggest that with Redgrave the tide of taste is slowly moving away from the romantic Hamlets of the past, especially the 1930s and 1940s. A more tough-minded Hamlet emerges. We can leave Redgrave with an analogy that, to one reviewer, suggested the ultimate category for the role: classicism. 'And whether by accident or design, this classicism gives us one unforgettable visual moment, when for "How all occasions do inform against me", he stands outlined against the cyclorama sky looking breath-takingly like the Lawrence portrait of Kemble as Hamlet, and just as majestic.'[15]

IV

The Hamlet of Peter O'Toole (1963) is worth glancing at, not because it was an outstandingly memorable or radically new creation but because of its circumstances. This was the play chosen to inaugurate the National Theatre in 1963; it was mounted by Sir Laurence Olivier, newly appointed to direct the National Theatre, and displayed the most admired and publicized young actor in the land. It is fair, then, to regard this *Hamlet* as a historic statement of what was considered possible and desirable to grace a long-awaited, famous occasion: the greatest play, the greatest playwright, the greatest actor-director, the finest young actor currently available. The world's spotlight was on the production, and good wishes assured in advance.

What did the director do? First, and above all, he chose to play an essentially uncut text. This excited little comment at the time, but it marks a profound shift in theatrical taste. The quest for *meaning*, the lodestone of the challenging RSC in the 1960s, entails an acquiescence in the total statement made by the total text. This was never a dogma; but the 1960s came to expect an exposure to the true text and not a series of expansive cuts, themselves stigmatized as 'traditional'. The prompt-text of the National Theatre *Hamlet* follows, in the main, the Second Quarto, the better text as scholars regard it. It is not necessary to follow the small cuts in detail. Twenty-four obscure lines on child actors go (II, ii, 338–61), as do a number of small additions found in the Folio but not in the Second Quarto. At the close the 'England' references and the English Ambassador's speech are cut (V, ii, 341, 344, 357–67) – conceivably some strange theatrical superstition in view of the circumstances. But, as a general description, this is as near as makes no difference an uncut Second Quarto playing-text. The only real liberty is to stage the soliloquies in the First Quarto order. This involves some shuffling around, so that 'To be or not to be' precedes the 'nunnery' scene. This was not controversial, and J. C. Trewin found the movement 'plain and logical'.[16]

The critics, while full of good wishes, were aware that they had not seen a great Hamlet. 'One should not think first of a *Hamlet* for its visual qualities.'[17] The *New Statesman* describes them at length. 'Desmond Heeley's costumes are a handsome jumble: mostly rich gold-encrusted Caroline, with flashes of Elizabethan (Osric in a flurry of bum-freezing mantles) or 19th century (hunting-habits for the ladies, with smooth Young-Victoria or Lampedusa-period hair-dos).'[18] To the *Spectator* critic, the court suggested the Field of the Cloth of

Gold, and the royal entrance a Velasquez scene. But he found Sean Kenny's set ugly. 'The set immediately obtrudes. A central arch and a thin ramp on the left rises to the full height of the stage. . . .'[19] And he drew the conclusion that 'this is grand opera. It is a spectacle. . . . Peter O'Toole was the *Heldentenor* to suit this interpretation. . . .'[20] One suspects that this shaft is not far off target: the entire occasion has more than a whiff of the Salzburg Festspielhaus. But Harold Hobson gave the performance a fairly clean bill of health: 'It is clear that Sir Laurence has directed Peter O'Toole to give a straightforward performance relying on force of acting instead of ingenious and unexpected renderings of the text. . . . Everything is subordinated to giving a swift and vivid picture of an exciting and thrilling play; and the acting fully substantiates the director's purpose.'[21] All the same, Roger Gellert found the performance unsatisfactory:

> Sir Laurence Olivier, who produced and evidently prefers blond Hamlets, speaks in a programme note of his belief in Hamlet as an Angry, eschewing both charm and the notion of a romantic weakling. But the bearing of O'Toole . . . flatly contradicts this intention, for he presents a soppily traditional creature, ravaged and suffused with self-pity. . . . Far from suggesting banked-up anger, he looks ready to blub at any moment. He is, in fact, the most limp-wristed Hamlet of recent years.[22]

This is highly adverse, and he concludes, after detailed praise for the company (especially Rosemary Harris' Ophelia), with 'For a princeless *Hamlet*, it isn't half bad, and we look to have the basis of a good National Company. It is, all the same, a disappointment.'[23] Probably it is soundest to stay with the more tempered reservations of J. C. Trewin: 'It is, in sum, a Hamlet without vocal warmth; a man of authority who does not command. . . .'[24] O'Toole, it would seem, did not for all his talents take the Hamlet citadel by storm; and the production over all, with its sumptuous costumes and Sean Kenny's brutalist set, appears an amalgam of period tastes. But the unfussy adherence to the superior text deserved more acclaim than it got. The movement in taste was steadily bearing *Hamlet* towards its 1960s apotheosis.

V

And this, undoubtedly, was David Warner's Hamlet of 1965 and 1966, directed by Peter Hall, at Stratford and the Aldwych. This was the culmination, as it now seems, of Hall's reign at the RSC: the occasion when he brought together the actor, the part, the play, at the precise moment in cultural time when the originality of the conception would be at once controversial and acceptable. For this was a much-loved and much-attacked *Hamlet*. It was sensed widely that Peter Hall was mounting a sustained assault on a theatrical stereotype while mobilizing many supporters for the innovation. This was a turning-point in that explosively transitional era, a set-piece battle whose objective was to redefine the modern, the passé.

First, the text. The prompt-book reveals the Second Quarto as the basis for production; it is certainly reduced, but there is a fundamental distinction in approaches to cutting. One way is to excise parts and sections – the Polonius–Reynaldo scene, Cornelius and Voltimand, English Ambassador, and so on. The alternative is to 'thin' rather than 'cut' (in the first sense): one reduces elaborations but retains speeches and parts. The topic sentence, so to say, is retained while the remainder of the paragraph goes. This is the approach Hall employed. The traditional absentees listed above all found a place in his production; but a light, mobile regard for local slimming is observable all through. The soliloquies were played uncut – they really are not to be tampered with – but long speeches from the lesser dramatis personae were not granted extreme respect. So Claudius, for example, lost half of his ' 'Tis sweet and commendable' speech to Hamlet in I, ii, but the rhetoric (which is arguably a kind of coded Shakespearean stage direction) is clearly dispensable. Typical of Hall's methods is Laertes' long homily to Ophelia (I, iii, 10–44). Most of this goes, beginning with 'For nature crescent . . .': much of the speech is pure Elizabethan humbug in tone and trope, and the hard advice can be extracted. Self-indulgent rhetoric gets short shrift. Polonius, in the same vein, loses most of 'Ay, springes to catch woodcocks'. Again, in I, iv, Hamlet in his platform meditation loses two lines ('By the o'ergrowth of some complexion . . . forts of reason') which, rather meanderingly, at once elaborates and attenuates the sense. The last two lines of the same speech go, permitting it to end on the clear 'particular fault'. Such savings permit the director to retain most of the Polonius–Reynaldo dialogue (II, i). The thinning policy is evident in II, ii, where most of the child-actor material goes. ('These are now the fashion . . . brains': lines 349–67). Anything which impedes the clear line of thought is challenged: so Polonius, to Claudius, retains 'And I do think . . . that I have found the very cause of Hamlet's lunacy' (II, ii, 46–9) but loses the intermediary clause 'or else this brain of mine/Hunts not the train of policy so sure/As it hath used to . . .'. These are surely 'technical' cuts, aids to mobility and clarity; but more significant is the departure of most of the 'ambition' dialogue with Rosencrantz and Guildenstern (II, ii): the cut extends from 'which dreams indeed are ambition' to 'most dreadfully attended' (II, ii, 261–74). Evidently the idea is to down-play ambition as a motive, and this is crucial to the Warner–Hall concept of an *apathetic* Hamlet.

The dumb show is retained, though there are substantial cuts in the Player King and Player Queen dialogue. This is reasonable, as is the excision of passages like 'paddock, from a bat, a gib' from the 'bloat king' speech (how many in the audience would understand the terms?). Similarly, in the politic Claudius–Laertes discourse (IV, vii) it is noticeable that the clear flow of thought and exchange is not impeded by difficulties such as 'scrimers of their nation' or conceited elaboration like 'And to such wondrous doing brought his horse. . . . Come short of what he did' (IV, vii, 87–91). The final Act sees no great cuts. In V, i, Hamlet loses the 'lawyer' meditation and the 'Age is grown so picked' comment, but all else stays. In V, ii, Hamlet's account of his stratagem is thinned; and 'their defeat/Does by their own insinuation grow. . . . Of mighty opposites' is cut (lines 58–62). So does 'And is't not to be damned. . . . In further evil' go: perhaps damnation is not a live issue in this production. (As it was to be in the same company's 1970 production.) But the bill of indictment against Claudius stays. Besides some Osric dialogue, the Queen's request to Hamlet to 'use some gentle entertainment to Laertes' goes: this is probably significant, as the director is not stressing the mother-influence here. Thereafter there are light cuts only, and the English Ambassador, like Fortinbras, is uncut. In all, this is a fluent and consecutive playing-text; it places great stress on meaning and intelligibility, and does not seek to stray far from the contours of Shakespeare's design.

The impact of the Hamlet based on this text – the Hamlet claimant, as Miller would put it – is most easily discernible in J. C. Trewin's account:

> There are moments in the Royal Shakespeare Company's *Hamlet* at Stratford-upon-Avon when the Prince, his lank blond hair ruffled, a rust-red scarf looped about his neck, and his cloak rucked up like a belted grey mackintosh, reminds us of a drama student, or an inconspicuous under-graduate, or a worried young man leaving a coffee-bar in the King's Road. If (we murmur) there is one personage he does not resemble, it is Hamlet, Prince of Denmark. But here Peter Hall, the director, and David Warner who at 24 is the youngest man ever to play the part in a Stratford-upon-

Avon Festival, will say at once that Hamlet's aspect, his image, must change
with the changing periods; they will point to the score of earlier actors
pictured – all so differently – in the theatre programme.
This new Hamlet, they suggest, is the portrait for the present decade. Mr
Hall thinks that, for contemporary listeners, the play is about disillusionment, something that produces an apathy of the will so deep that
'commitment to politics, to religion, or to life is impossible'.[25]

The most contemporary of images, then. But this does not imply a too
overtly modernist production, as Robert Speaight has noted:

> If he were bent on an existentialist *Hamlet* – and the word can stand, though
> it has stood too long – Mr Hall may have been tempted to produce it in
> modern dress. Very wisely, he did not. It was essential to preserve the link
> between the time at which the play was written and the time in which it is
> being performed – between Montaigne's doubt and Pascal's anguish, and
> our own. There was no doubt that we were living under the shadow of
> Machiavelli, and the audience could decide according to their political
> sympathies whether they were also living under the shadow of Macmillan.
> The production, owing to Mr John Bury's saturnine imagination, had space
> and scale and splendour, but the splendour was not obtrusively baroque.
> Elsinore was not giving itself away so easily. Much better for Hamlet to
> scent the corruption under a façade of sobriety, because the point of the
> play is that he is the only one to smell it out; and Claudius is far too astute a
> man not to preserve the appearances. Mr Hall rightly saw that *Hamlet* is a
> personal tragedy in the context of a political melodrama, and nothing was
> better in this production than the quiet, efficient functioning of public life.
> The opening tableau of Act One, Scene ii – Claudius' first meeting with the
> Privy Council, with Hamlet imprisoned at the table – was far more telling
> than the ostentatious solitude in which he is usually set apart. That table
> was the cage of circumstance in which he was caught up, and only through
> his own death and the death of others would he be able to escape from it.[26]

So the contemporaneity is not crass, and to the *New Statesman* 'the
only Kott-marks on the production are the general, not specially
revolutionary notion of a young existentialist trapped by politics into a
bloody, uncongenial role, and an ambiguous burst of laughter (it can
be taken more specifically, and make more sense) by the dying prince
at the Absurdity of it all'. How does it all work? The persona thus
established is extraordinarily recognizable, and plausible:

> He shelters in childishness, seeking to appear not merely too insane to be
> responsible for his actions, but too young. His disguise is not just dishevel-
> ment, but the wilful untidiness of an undergraduate, the half-baked
> impertinence of the adolescent who would test his parents' love to the limit
> of tolerance. He slops ostentatiously through the castle in a greenish, moth-

eaten student's gown, peering owlishly over his spectacles to cheek his elders. He knows his position as heir to the throne protects him, and abuses it as far as he can. The easiest disguise for an adolescent with a problem too big for him is that of a problem adolescent.[27]

And this immaturity, in turn, has a most convincing psychological objective. It is his dead father who generates the mental drama, rather than the live mother:

> For the revenge he really wishes, and achieves, is on himself for not being the great Hamlet his father was. The key to every *Hamlet* is its ghost. A solid ghost demands an active, believing hero, thwarted by events; an insubstantial one, all light effects and echoes, a brainsick prince, nerveless and Oedipal. The apparition which swims above the walls of John Bury's Elsinore (a superb inferno of bitumen ramparts and lakes of black marble, whose throne-room swarms with faded frescoes of sad and grey Rubens flesh like a wax museum of elderly lasciviousness) is something new: a giant, helmeted shadow 10 feet tall which dwarfs his shuddering child in a dark, commanding embrace. 'This was a man,' Hamlet tells Horatio enviously: for once we are shown the other side of the Oedipus complex.[28]

The always-dependable judgement of Robert Speaight confirms the insight: 'You can almost divide Hamlets into those who are in love with their father and those who are in love with their mother. There is no doubt where Mr Warner stands, and I will swear that no Hamlet has made more moving an end.'[29]

The quality of acting, and more particularly the speaking of the soliloquies, is worth noting. This is how Trewin saw it:

> It is the voice of a baffled youth at war with himself, caught in the busy 'prison' that is Denmark, unable to urge himself to action, finding that he has a way of expressing himself poetically, and shying from the idea in embarrassment. He will argue closely and very, very slowly, with himself and with the members of the audience he is anxious to draw into his soliloquies ('Am I a coward?').[30]

And Ronald Bryden:

> This is a Hamlet desperately in need of counsel, help, experience, and he actually seeks it from the audience in his soliloquies. That is probably the greatest triumph of the production: using the Elizabethan convention with total literalness, Hamlet communes not with himself but with you. For the first time in my experience, the rhetoric, spoken as it was intended to be, comes brilliantly to life.[31]

A uniquely involving, astonishingly immediate Hamlet, this: the charge of 'maturity' against earlier Hamlets has been completely inverted. But, naturally, all this was achieved at a cost. The almost complete absence of the traditional Hamlet qualities – conventional good-looks, stylish deportment, 'nobility' in short – came as a shock to many. It is true that, as Ronald Bryden put it in his afterthoughts on the 1966 production, 'People have complained of this Hamlet's lack of nobility. Nobility is a quality which excludes a good many others.'[32] Granted, but the loss is still there. The *Spectator* critic found it all completely inadequate:

> He is very young, very impressed by Mr Bob Dylan, very much a product of the new RADA. His Hamlet's 'antic disposition' consists of spectacles, a kind of mackintosh and a long red muffler to hide the dangerous romantic associations of a bare throat. His Hamlet, perhaps a coward, certainly a pacifist, bites his nails, scratches his face during a soliloquy, wipes his brow from time to time, is clean-shaven quite against the text. 'Oh vengeance!' he cries in a tiny, tinny voice. In short, he is anti-heroic, anti-romantic and very suitably the subject of the shrill pre-pubescent ecstasy in the gallery.[33]

And Trewin had to confess his distaste for 'Hamlet's relentless scruffiness': 'The trouble is that we, too, are progressively disillusioned as a great part shrinks to the proportions deemed to be modish in 1965, and as the great lines fail to ring.'[34]

Still, the final moments of the production saved everything, even for the doubters. One critic describes it thus:

> And I shall remember the strange final scene when (after the ferocious duel) Hamlet thrusts the poisoned cup upon the king and stands laughing at the death-throes. It is over now; he moves around with a dazed smile of triumph, relief that his task is done, that action has been forced upon him. Presently, as the poison works, he has to sink upon a bench, but the look of triumph remains upon his face as he kisses his father's miniature and fades into death, leaving Horatio to report him to the world. Nothing becomes the performance like its end.[35]

And Robert Speaight elaborates it for us:

> But the merit of Mr Warner's Hamlet is that it is too young and too fresh to have any memories of its own. He does these things and says these things because, as far as he is concerned, no one has ever said or done them before. The result is that even the oldest of us feel that we are seeing the play for the first time. He is casual where other actors are emphatic, and emphatic where they are casual. Nowhere was this originality more impressive than in his final speech. 'Well, there you are', he seemed to be saying, 'all this

trouble began with my father's row with old Fortinbras, and here is young Fortinbras arriving in the nick of time to pay off old scores. Pretty funny, isn't it? Never mind, I suppose they'll all vote for him, and I'd vote for him too.' And then, the single touch of uncomplicated sentiment saved up for the last moment of all, when he kisses his father's miniature – father and son 'folded into the constitution of silence'.[36]

Anti-heroic, anti-romantic it may have been, but the great play triumphantly survived in this presentation. The doubts about the Hamlet will remain; but the verdict on the whole may well rest with another Stratford director, as expressed to me: 'The best *production* of *Hamlet* I ever saw.' In its way, this is certainly a supreme achievement, as it is a litmus, of the 1960s.

VI

Nevertheless, the movement of time had supplied an additional critique to the Hall–Warner *Hamlet* by the end of the decade, when Trevor Nunn directed the RSC production with Alan Howard in the lead. The changed world of 1970 accounts for the points made by the previous director, Peter Hall, in an interview about this time:

One lives in one's own time and cannot escape it. We don't even know what an Elizabethan interpretation of Hamlet *was* . . . you should approach a classic with the maximum of scholarship you can muster – and then you honestly try to interpret what you think it means to a person living now. . . . Given 1965, the RSC, its audience, all one's knowledge of *Hamlet* – we showed what had to emerge. I saw *Hamlet* as a very political play. . . . Equally, I remembered that in 1965 one thought that the young were very very misunderstood by their elders. We thought them beautiful, tolerant, quiet. They were flower children whose very generosity at times seemed to be apathy. One couldn't get them to react to very much . . . there *is* apathy in *Hamlet* – he feels that the older generation have betrayed him.[37]

The point being, naturally, that between 1966 and 1970 stood 1968. The 'apathy' that Hall (and many others) saw in the student generation of the early sixties gave way to the activism of the late sixties.[38] Thus, the fumbling graduate student located in the physical image of David Warner was already a period piece: *les èvènements de mai* announced a situation in which student-Hamlets were to do *something* about their society. The text of *Hamlet*, none the less, remained to be expounded; and the talents of the leading young actor of the RSC were put at the disposal of Trevor Nunn's exposition.

The text, though not heavily cut, was fairly extensively thinned. Robert Speaight considered that

> Mr Nunn's cuts are always rational. They made sense, but in Shakespeare music and meaning are one. . . . Shakespeare's repetitions and elaborations of a thought or a theme are as much a part of his method as similar repetitions and elaborations in music, and they resist amputation. I could have spared, on the other hand, much more of Osric; and I thought the end of the play could have been further shortened, and the pace of the last two acts very considerably speeded up.[39]

To take some instances, in the first scene the director presents a concrete, un-spooky Ghost. However, Horatio's 'Most like' answer goes, as does 'Together with that fair and warlike form': Nunn treats the lines as a stage direction, which needs only to be *implemented* not spoken. There are some standard cuts from the rhetoric of Claudius ('Tis sweet and commendable') and the homilies of Laertes and Polonius; the child-actor allusions of II, ii are much reduced; rather surprisingly, Hamlet loses much of his advice to the Players. The dumb show stays, and Player King and Player Queen suffer such cuts that 'Our wills and fates . . . none of our own' becomes virtually a motto-statement, the scaffolding round it having collapsed. One is glad to report that Hamlets are no longer too sensitive to 'lug the guts into the neighbour room'. The opening of V, ii, though a little thinned, is substantially intact. The scene does start with 'So much for this, sir'; 'Ere I could make a prologue' stays, a necessary testimony to the histrionic side of Hamlet; 'So Rosencrantz and Guildenstern go to it' to 'the portraiture of his' is uncut, a vital exposition. Curiously, the lines on 'the bravery of his grief' go; one would have thought that the rival-Thespian aspect was worth retaining. A textual interpretation at this point is worth recording: at 'A man's life's no more than to say "One" ', stage directions in the prompt-book give *'Hamlet drinks Horatio drinks'*. (Is one to take 'One' as the Renaissance equivalent of 'skol'?) The English Ambassador, sadly, disappears, and Horatio answers Fortinbras' question with 'give order that . . .'. Fortinbras' final speech loses 'And for his passage/The soldier's music and the rites of war/Speak loudly for him'.

Critics and public received this *Hamlet* with respect, but without great controversy or acclaim. Perhaps 1970 was something of a lull in cultural time. The setting, certainly, was ultra-fashionable:

> Trevor Nunn's production of *Hamlet* is set by Christopher Morley on a bare stage in black and white and monochrome. The players' dresses – blue and

orange, green and scarlet on their gaudy painted stage – are the first and only colours in this production. A flood of bleached and weathered wooden boards shelves steeply up to meet a white, sloping, slated roof. A narrow wall of black slats at the back divides the two. Trapped between the tilted roof and floor, boxed in on either side by high, black, slatted walls, is a great airy empty space: Mr Morley has built not so much a stage-set as a theatre, a receptacle to hold a play.[40]

The *theatricality* of the design is central to the concept. As a context for the tactics of production, it worked beautifully:

> And, for ceremony and spectacle, this setting has a splendour which – precisely because it escapes entirely the painted scenery and chiaroscuro lighting of nineteenth century theatre – stretches back to an older, more rhetorical tradition: light spills down on the massed court, standing shoulder to shoulder and perfectly motionless in heavy, white, furred robes, and on Claudius' coarse, staring face as he delivers his first speeches in the tones, at once unctuous and hectoring, of a politician at a public meeting. Hard to convey the magnificence and the menacing bleakness of this scene, or, for that matter, the electric brilliance of the final duel . . . between Hamlet and Laertes, whipping over the stage in great arcs and arabesques between courtiers posed massively, like boulders, on a bare, chalky ground.[41]

The Stratford 'white box' allows a concentration on local or timeless resonances: 'As a large, browning map behind them confirms, we are presumably to remember that the action occurs in the northern country, not so far from the Arctic Circle. Quite where this aperçu gets us is hard to say. . . .'[42] *Pace* the *New Statesman* here, it seems likely that a masculine, a male-oriented society is projected with a particular area of alienation in mind.

Alan Howard's Hamlet stems from a distinguished presence and a considerable intelligence, and Speaight found it 'in line with other classical interpretations of the part.'[43] It was, for him, rooted in the shock of Claudius' marriage to Gertrude. 'The assumption of madness was felt as an escape from an intolerable sanity; and when Hamlet stabbed Polonius – not once but over and over again – you remembered the frustration of "and can do *nothing*".'[44] J. C. Trewin found him a 'manic-depressive',[45] and D. A. N. Jones, interestingly, saw the role as tied to Howard's own upbringing:

> Alan Howard, who plays Hamlet, was brought up in the Outer Hebrides, and acts as if he were fey – 'fated soon to die, often marked by extravagantly high spirits'. As in other productions, this tall, wild-eyed man expresses easily that amoral wantonness which, in children, we call innocence, and his voice slides into a faraway, muted tone, like a child telling ghost stories. He is eerie and quaint.[46]

Benedict Nightingale advances the line that Hamlet is decisively drama-oriented, a pillar of the Wittenberg University Drama Society. This emerges in his relations with the Players, naturally. 'Poor wretch, he has found himself suddenly cast as leading man in an infinitely complex drama, and without a script. Where and how is he to improvise?'[47] This is tied in with an emphasis on the theological side, something that permits the director to make the most of a theatrical opportunity:

> Nunn, too, goes out of his way to remind us that Hamlet lives in a nominally Christian society, which can scarcely sanction the taking of uncles for fathers, or not without absolute proof of capital guilt. Hamlet and Horatio wear crosses throughout; Hamlet consigns Ophelia to a nunnery while they're sitting together in a pew in the Palace chapel, overheard by Claudius and Polonius in a nearby confessional; hooded monks file past, ringing bells, and Hamlet himself puts on a cowl before visiting Gertrude. This impersonation is partly a symptom of his histrionic instincts – he can best harrow and shrive his mother if he's in the right costume – and partly a reminder of the moral and spiritual values a prince is supposed to endorse.[48]

Undoubtedly, this emphasis – which the prompt-book bears out – on monks, confessionals, pews and crosses reminds us of a dimension of the inner drama almost always ignored today. The awareness of 'theological' drama is rather a trademark of the RSC (cf. Nunn's Christian *Macbeth*) than a broad modern tendency.

Over all, one gleans from the reviews a vague dissatisfaction: a recognition that this was an intelligent, well-graced and capable Hamlet, but whose conception was not projected with crystalline precision and which, moreover, left the audience not totally moved at the end. Perhaps this is the direction in which modernist *Hamlets* are moving: that the former great weight of the production upon one actor is being redistributed. This would harmonize with a movement of the times, to value the ensemble above the 'star' vehicle. And this leaves space for other vistas to emerge. We can end with the view of a critic who comes close to saying that the play is not even Hamlet's tragedy:

> Hamlet has, as she says, cleft her heart in twain: she's become a glazed mask of a woman, anaesthetized, almost catatonic, unable to react to anyone or anything. Perhaps she realises she married a murderer, perhaps not. Perhaps she guesses that the cup is poisoned, perhaps not. The production points gently, and hints, no more. But she dies gratefully enough, and Claudius, who does not wish to survive her, follows her willingly, almost eagerly. Myself, I found the suicide of this bad, vulnerable, pathetic couple more moving than the conventional death of Howard's Hamlet.[49]

Something of the uncertainty of our times has communicated itself to *Hamlet*. The productions of late years show no commanding principle or direction, and one could illustrate various theses from the stage instances. Peter Hall's production for the National Theatre (1976), with Albert Finney in the lead, was formally notable. Yet there was support for Irving Wardle's disenchanted view: 'Ten years ago when Mr Hall directed the play at Stratford . . . the tragedy swung round and confronted us like a great dark mirror. . . . Whatever the claims of the new version, it throws back no reflection of that sort. It is a ponderous cultural event which will attract the star-following public and gratify spectators of the "Shakespearian intentions" school. I can recall few productions less coloured by a directorial viewpoint.'[50] A full-text version (that is, a conflation of Second Quarto and Folio) is always welcome; yet it seemed in 1976 less an affirmation of the text's integrity than a slightly limp invitation to the public to find what it could perceive in the *Rohrschach*. Finney played the part for energy and vitality, without discernible concept.[51] Bernard Crick dismissed him thus: 'Albert Finney's Hamlet is . . . a quite straightforward Fortinbras.'[52]

Then again, Toby Robertson's production for the Prospect Theatre (1977) seemed an exercise in de-romanticizing the part. 'Derek Jacobi's Hamlet is certainly no hero . . . he is a show-off . . . a juvenile hypocrite. . . . Of course, he is deferential about his fencing skills: he knows he can beat Laertes. Starting as underdog is more dramatic.'[53] Hamlet did, however, regain some of his princely qualities: 'Derek Jacobi restores the figure of the Renaissance prince, apt to break into falsetto hysterics under stress, but equipped with all the courtesy, irony and masterful variations of tempo and weight that traditionally belong to the part.'[54] But here, as earlier, one notices a perhaps ominous sign of the times: Claudius scores well against Hamlet. Timothy West (Prospect Theatre, 1977) Denis Quilley (National Theatre, 1977) and David Waller (RSC, 1970), for instance, received virtually unanimous praise. In contemporary stage dynamics, for whatever reasons, Claudius is highly playable.[55] This fact lends itself to a de-romanticized view of Hamlet.[56] The contemporary perception of *Hamlet* is far from an acquiescence in the claims made by its star.

Scepticism and uncertainty: Hamlets can scarcely hope to escape their social and historical fate. Their responses will have to be intuitive, pragmatic, variable. And in this they will mirror the problem contained in the great text. When Robin Phillips directed the play at Stratford, Ontario, in 1976, he assigned the lead to two actors in alternation: Richard Monette and Nicholas Pennell. They have since let it be known[57] that their chief problem was during rehearsal: the immense psychological difficulty of going on to rehearse, with the same supporting actors, a scene in which their alternate had preceded them. And this is not unlike the original problem of Hamlet, who has to improvise on a role handed down to him from his father. (In the end, Phillips solved the directorial problem by insisting that Monette and Pennell attend each other's rehearsals.) There was no identity of approach to the part. Pennell chose to orient his interpretation towards Gertrude, Monette towards Hamlet senior.[58] One could do worse than take the Ontario experience as an action emblem of *Hamlet* in the 1970s.

NOTES

1 John Elsom, *Postwar British Theatre* (London: Routledge & Kegan Paul, 1976), p. 34.
2 Robert Speaight, 'Shakespeare in Britain', *Shakespeare Quarterly*, vol. XVII (1966), p. 394.
3 John Gielgud, *Stage Directions* (London: Heinemann, 1963), p. 37.
4 John Russell Brown, 'The Royal Shakespeare Company 1965', *Shakespeare Survey 19* (1966), p. 113.
5 T. C. Worsley, *New Statesman*, 1 May 1948.
6 John Garrett, *The Spectator*, 30 April 1948.
7 J. C. Trewin, *Shakespeare on the English Stage 1900–1964* (London: Barrie & Rockliff, 1964), p. 194. The production was George Rylands'. Desmond MacCarthy found the Elsinore setting 'hardly more stimulating to the imagination than a dismal, mid-Victorian Gothic hydro'. He thought Gielgud 'better at conveying Hamlet's conscious weakness (in swallowing tears) than the rasp of his intellectual irony' (*New Statesman*, 21 October 1944). For a full account of Gielgud's Hamlet, see Rosamond Gilder, *John Gielgud's Hamlet* (London: Methuen, 1937).
8 M. St Clare Byrne, 'The Shakespeare season at the Old Vic, 1975–58, and Stratford-upon-Avon, 1958', *Shakespeare Quarterly*, vol. IX (1958), p. 518.
9 T. C. Worsley, *New Statesman*, 21 June 1958.
10 Alan Brien, *The Spectator*, 13 June 1958.
11 T. C. Worsley, *New Statesman*, 21 June 1958.
12 Ralph Berry, *On Directing Shakespeare: Interviews with Contemporary Directors* (London and New York: Croom Helm and Barnes & Noble, 1977), p. 38.
13 Byrne, op. cit., p. 516.
14 Ibid.
15 Ibid.
16 J. C. Trewin, *The Illustrated London News*, 2 November 1963.
17 Ibid.
18 Roger Gellert, *New Statesman*, 1 November 1963.
19 David Pryce-Jones, *The Spectator*, 1 November 1963.
20 Ibid.
21 Harold Hobson, '*Hamlet* at the National Theatre', *The Listener*, 7 November 1963.

22 Gellert, op. cit.
23 Ibid.
24 J. C. Trewin, *The Illustrated London News*, 2 November 1963.
25 J. C. Trewin, 'Mr Hall and Mr Warner find a Hamlet image for 1965', *The Illustrated London News*, 28 August 1965.
26 Robert Speaight, 'Shakespeare in Britain', *Shakespeare Quarterly*, vol. XVI (1965), p. 320.
27 Ronald Bryden, *New Statesman*, 27 August 1965.
28 Ibid.
29 Speaight, *Shakespeare Quarterly*, vol. XVI, pp. 321–2.
30 Trewin, *The Illustrated London News*, 28 August 1965.
31 Ronald Bryden, *New Statesman*, 27 August 1965.
32 Ronald Bryden, *New Statesman*, 7 January 1966.
33 David Pryce-Jones, *The Spectator*, 27 August 1965.
34 Trewin, *The Illustrated London News*, 28 August 1965.
35 Ibid.
36 Speaight, *Shakespeare Quarterly*, vol. XVI, p. 321.
37 Peter Hall, 'Director in interview', *Plays and Players* (June 1970). Quoted in David Addenbrooke, *The Royal Shakespeare Company* (London: William Kimber, 1974), p. 129. In 1965, Hall had been certain in his linking of Hamlet's spiritual condition with apathy among the young. 'For our decade I think the play will be about the disillusionment which produces an apathy of the will so deep that commitment to politics, to religion or to life is impossible'. (Stanley Wells, *Royal Shakespeare: Four Major Productions at Stratford-upon-Avon* (Manchester: Manchester University Press, 1977), p. 25).
38 The *Glasgow Herald* reviewer (9 June 1970) found Hamlet 'a student demonstrator, fresh from Wittenberg'. Frank Marcus (*Sunday Telegraph*, 7 June 1970) saw him as 'the prototypical student demonstrator, a bit scruffy, sitting naturally on the floor, and blowing raspberries'.
39 Robert Speaight, 'Shakespeare in Britain', *Shakespeare Quarterly*, vol. XXI (1970), pp. 442–3.
40 Hilary Spurling, *The Spectator*, 13 June 1970.
41 Ibid.
42 Benedict Nightingale, *New Statesman*, 12 June 1970.
43 Speaight, *Shakespeare Quarterly*, vol. XXI, p. 444.
44 Ibid., p. 443. Ronald Bryden's review (*The Observer*, 7 June 1970) stresses the idea of alienation: 'He [Nunn] didn't mention R. D. Laing, but this should go down as the Laingian Hamlet. . . . Hamlet was a study of alienation. . . . His madness is not just feigned, it is a Laingian escape from a society built on lunatic deceptions into the lonely sanity of private truth.' Bryden was present at a number of rehearsals, and was thus more thoroughly imbued with the production's concepts than other reviewers.
45 J. C. Trewin, *The Illustrated London News*, 20 June 1970.
46 D. A. N. Jones, *The Listener*, 11 June 1970.
47 Nightingale, op. cit. Irving Wardle concurs with Nightingale's view: 'he is throughout an improvising actor. There is no moment when he talks on level human terms or says anything straight' (*The Times*, 5 June 1970).
48 Nightingale, op. cit.
49 Ibid.
50 Irving Wardle, *The Times*, 11 December 1975.

51 'He cuts out pathos, reflective philosophy, and melancholy; and bases his per-
    formance on energy, bluff comradeship, and sardonic derision' (Irving Wardle, *The
    Times*, 11 December 1975).

52 Bernard Crick, *The Times Higher Educational Supplement*, 13 February 1976.

53 John Elsom, *The Listener*, 9 June 1977. One sometimes wonders if a decisive event
    in *Hamlet* studies was not the publication of Stephen Potter's *Gamesmanship*.

54 Irving Wardle, *The Times*, 31 May 1977.

55 It may be true that Claudius is simply getting more lines. The productions of 1948,
    1958 and 1966 each cut about 100 lines from Claudius' part; but the RSC pro-
    duction of 1970 left Claudius all but intact.

56 The anti-romantic Hamlet is now an orthodoxy. I should have liked to have seen
    the German Hamlet, Ulrich Wildgruber, who really was fat and scant of breath.
    See Werner Habicht, 'Shakespeare in West Germany', *Shakespeare Quarterly*, vol.
    XXIX (1978), p. 298. As I go to press, the latest Hamlet, Jonathan Pryce's (Royal
    Court, directed by Richard Eyre), is distinguished for outrageous conduct. Francis
    King (*Sunday Telegraph*, 6 April 1980) saw in him 'the growing insanity of a man-
    child who prefers to go mad than to be forced to grow up. A gangling, twitching
    neurasthenic, he seethes with an inner chaos that threatens the precarious order of
    an adult world of complacence, concealment and compromise.' Robert Cushman
    (*The Observer*, 6 April 1980) compares Pryce with the David Warner of 1965: 'Mr
    Warner was acclaimed less as an actor than as an archetype; he was taken to be the
    essence of studenthood, 1965. The interest attaching to Mr Pryce is more strictly
    gladiatorial: that of seeing a prized young actor, not in himself particularly repre-
    sentative of anything, match his own talent to the role. . . . It is odd, considering
    what they have to put up with from him, how much everyone in the play likes
    Hamlet. Nobody – except Claudius when lying and Laertes when duped – ever
    says a word against him. Mr Pryce's power and intelligence are amply backed up
    by sheer cheek. . . .'

57 At, for example, a session of the Shakespeare Association of America conference:
    Toronto, 15 April 1978.

58 *Hamlet* seems at last to be moving away from the Oedipal fixation. A recent book
    argues strongly that Hamlet's father is his most important influence: see Avi
    Erlich, *Hamlet's Absent Father* (Princeton, NJ: Princeton University Press, 1977).

CHAPTER SIX

The Season of
Twelfth Night

Twelfth Night is the statutory comedy, as often as not, in a summer festival season. Any moderately dedicated playgoer must have seen it several times, and passed up many more chances. Like *Hamlet*, it tends to be absorbed into the general textures of the current theatre, and it is not usually associated with revolutionary productions. Moreover, it is not the focus of any great academic or theatrical debate. Its meaning is not in doubt: *Twelfth Night* is widely accepted as a supreme harmonizing of the romantic and the comic, sweet and astringent. The admirable production, then, is held to be one which holds these elements in balance. It is in the inflection which a production gives to *Twelfth Night* that the special interest lies. And this inflection has undoubtedly modulated in recent years. Broadly, and crudely: *Twelfth Night* used to be funny, and is now much less so. What has happened?

I want to describe two models of *Twelfth Night* productions, old and new. The seamless fabric of theatre history does not lend itself to radical departures, yet I think I can point to a date for the founding of the New Model *Twelfth Night*: 1969. For the old, I shall turn to the late nineteenth century, and synthesize a few productions. This is less for their antiquarian interest than for their continuing influence. The nineteenth century reveals in caricatured form contours of a *Twelfth Night* that were recognizable until quite recently, and are still visible in the outer provinces of theatre.

I

The essence of the old model was its direct appeal to laughter and romance. Of Augustin Daly's production in New York, 1894, Odell tells us: 'Moonlight was brought into play as never before in this comedy; Viola dreamed on a bench as Orsino's minstrels warbled Shubert's [sic] "Who is Olivia (Sylvia)?"'[1] *The New York Herald-Tribune* has this:

> The scene is Olivia's garden. The time is evening. Viola, disguised as the minstrel Cesario, having received an intimation that perhaps her brother, Sebastian, has not drowned, has spoken her joyous soliloquy upon that auspicious thought, and has sunk into a seat, in meditation. The moon is rising over the distant sea, and in the fancied freshness of the balmy rising breeze you can almost hear the ripple of the leaves. The lovelorn Orsino enters, with many musicians, and they sing a serenade, beneath the windows of Olivia's palace. The proud beauty comes forth upon her balcony, and parting her veil, looks down upon Viola. . . . Not a word is spoken and not a word is needed. The garden is all in moonlight; the delicious music flows on; and . . . the curtain slowly falls. It was a perfect triumph of art, in the highest and best vein.[2]

It is, however, through the appeal to laughter that this piece must be gauged. The old prompt-books give us a fair idea of the mechanisms of production.

Take the great drinking scene (II, iii). The main thrust of production was to play up the drinking, singing and general merriment. The standard stage direction was *'Table and 3 chairs discovered. Tankards and long clay pipes on tables'*.[3] Feste, incredibly, might be the life and soul of the party. *'Clown jumps over table, and all three dance in circle.'*[4] Some interpolated songs were usual. Sir Andrew sang 'Christmas comes but once a year/And therefore we'll be merry'[5] after the catch, which has the double effect of defining the title more closely and allying it with the spirit of simple revelry. This spirit dominated the scene's end. A hallowed interpolation (after 'Come, knight') was

Sir Andrew:	Sunday, Monday, Tuesday,
	Which is the properest day to drink?
Sir Andrew:	
Sir Toby:	This is the properest day to drink!
Clown.	

Note the upbeat ending, after Shakespeare has written in a downbeat cadence (matching the opening). Henry Jewett's production (Boston, 1915) went farther, with much business of people sliding around in the dark, falling candles, and the ominous direction *'MUSIC PIANO JOVIAL'*.[6] The general commitment to revelry was unquestioned.

This comes out, naturally, in the garden scene (II, v). This scene has to be played quite straightforwardly for laughter: as one prompt has it, '*Bns of Bobbing from behind Trees all thro' this*'.⁷ But the ruthless insistence of the Neilson prompt on the laugh-quota is interesting. After Malvolio's exit from the garden the play-text reads: '*Omnes*. Ha! ha! ha!' (shades of Greyfriars). And following Maria's entrance and Sir Toby's 'Wilt thou set thy foot o' my neck?' '*all laugh and keep it up as long as possible*'. There is a similar instruction to Fabian after Malvolio's cross-gartered scene. It is really an anticipation of canned laughter. Fabian is the audience's stalking-horse, and he dramatizes the risibility of the play.

There is, I think, a hint of realization by the directors that the laughter-elements need to be 'protected' or played up. There is no real need for cuts aimed at shortening the piece – *Twelfth Night* is not long – so all cuts tend to reveal a shaping impulse. Sir Toby's 'I would we were well rid of this knavery. If he may be conveniently delivered, I would he were, for I am now so far in offence with my niece that I cannot pursue with any safety this sport to the upshot' (IV, ii, 72–6) disappears from Irving's prompt.⁸ Thus, a singularly unpleasant passage, which markedly qualifies our view of Sir Toby as a jolly dog, yields in the interests of a rounded stereotype.

Malvolio presents a central challenge to Sir Toby's view of the action, and solutions vary. Irving played his virtually uncut, taking his chances for pathos for all they were worth. (He notes '*crying*' in his prompt for 'Ay, good fool' in the prison scene.) Daly cut Malvolio totally from the fifth Act; the prison scene was his last. But cuts in Malvolio's final appearance were common. Neilson cut his 'And tell me, in the modesty of honour' to 'That e'er invention played on? Tell me why!' Olivia's 'Alas, poor fool, how have they baffled thee' goes, together with Feste's bitter 'whirligig of time' speech: thus, some painful elements are expunged. Malvolio's 'I'll be revenged on the whole pack of you' is in response to Fabian's 'on both sides passed'. This shows an awareness of the problem. Feste is to be 'protected' against his own words, and Malvolio is less pathetic – the fewer words he has, the less poignant his plight is.

As so often in the nineteenth century, Feste's 'whirligig of time' speech seems to have been felt rather strong, even though elsewhere a coarse communal sensibility is evident. Neilson, as we have seen, cut it. Jewett left it in, but followed Feste's 'revenges' with '*Laugh. Bus. Mal. down C. and turn up tear off chains. Mal. music for exit.*' 'Malvolio music. . . .' Still, the direction identifies the problem.

The conclusion formalizes the old view of *Twelfth Night*. It was customary to interpolate these lines for the Duke (after Malvolio's exit):

And now after twelve nights of tastes and pleasures,
Let me commend you to your dancing measures.

A dance followed. Thus, an invocation to revelry, and *not* Feste's
downbeat 'When that I was and a little tiny boy', ended the play. In
short, the old model took every opportunity to play up the farcical and
comic elements; it softened the asperities of Malvolio's humiliation; it
projected, finally, an apotheosis of romance, good-humour and social
accord. But it strained somewhat at the text to achieve these effects.
One senses a directorial awareness that the play is not so easy, or so
reassuring, as all that.

II

The new model, to my observation, starts edging into view in the
1950s. Historically, I am content to relate it to the profound shift in
sensibility which occurred in the English theatre around 1956.[9] of
course one can find earlier evidence of productions with modernist
elements, of a performance (say) that restored Sir Toby to the
knighthood.[10] Such a one was Granville-Barker's at the Savoy (1912),
a production 'unimpeded by detail [which] allowed the creative artifice
of its conception to do its work'.[11] But this play gathers business
relentlessly,[12] and Sir Toby is prone to relapses: his surname,
historically, weighs down his title. For all Granville-Barker's
innovations, the old model was still recognizable into modern times.
Hugh Hunt's production at the old Vic (1950) and John Gielgud's at
Stratford (1955) with Olivier as Malvolio can be thought of as a
culmination of the earlier type. They were refinements of a traditional
perception of the text. After the Gielgud *Twelfth Night*, one can
observe the scene changing. I limit my case here to a couple of critical
reactions. So intelligent a critic as Laurence Kitchin writes (in 1960),
'*Twelfth Night*, even in the drinking scene, is not farce'.[13] He would
not have needed to say that a few years later. One locates social time
through the démodé, and Muriel St Clare Byrne is especially dismissive of an Old Vic production that got it wrong. 'Farcical' is the
word that recurs in her long review.[14] Malvolios who cross-garter both
legs together will no longer do.

That was in 1958. In the same year Peter Hall, as we should expect,
got it right. His Stratford production was costumed in a Cavalier style
that suggested, a shade ominously, Van Dyck. Robert Speaight took
the point: 'Mr Hall had conceived his Illyria in some English autumn

not too long before the outbreak of the Civil War'.[15] *Autumn* is, conceptually, the key word: it comprehends the gold and russet-brown of Lila de Nobili's set, and the subliminal notion of nostalgia for the golden age, the pastoral *ante-bellum* world. 'What luckless apple did we taste,/To make us mortal, and thee waste?' Years after, Hall's successor at the RSC, Trevor Nunn, had no doubt that this *Twelfth Night* was 'definitively right. He had touched a Chekhov-like centre in the play; it was unarguable.'[16] Yet at the time critics felt that Hall's casting took certain liberties. The focus of displeasure was Geraldine McEwan's Olivia. This actress has since become best known as a comedy-of-manners specialist – she has played very successfully in Congreve, Lonsdale, Maugham, for instance – and her *poseuse* Olivia, complete with giggles and squeaks, undercut the Romantic tradition.[17] Olivias used to be played in the County Matron manner. For the rest, Sir Toby (Patrick Wymark) was a gentleman. (To take Sir Toby seriously is a sign of a modern production.) Malvolio (Eric Porter) was a recognizable human being. Above all, Max Adrian's intelligent and melancholy Feste dominated the play. His final envoi was 'a distant and elegant pavane'.[18]

The casting of *Twelfth Night* is open to a wide variety of options; the text is extraordinarily elastic.[19] I don't want to discuss these options in detail, but I stress the dualism of the matter: *Belch* (with its humours, stereotypic suggestion) or *Sir Toby*. (We could remember Elgar's epigraph for his *Falstaff*, 'a knight, a gentleman, and a soldier'.) Olivia plays well as a *grande dame* or as an aristocratic *ingénue*. More than that, some parts seem designed as functional variables, as spaces left open for the director to fill. Fabian is the leading instance. Neutral and unaligned, he can be played old or young, penny plain or tuppence coloured, English or Welsh ('I would exult, *mun*'). Maria, as we shall see, turns out to be another variable. But any discussion of individual parts is apt to miss the point. The point lies in the constellation of relationships, in the overall system of checks and balances. If you want a melancholy Feste, someone has to cheer us up; if you plan a bleak *Twelfth Night*, you need a Feste with vivacity.

And that leads us to the initial production of the contemporary era, John Barton's RSC production of 1969 (revived in 1971).[20] Much admired and much contested, this is a directorial statement that rests solidly on the title: *Twelfth Night*. It is curious that this has been so widely interpreted as an unequivocal call to revelry. In fact, most people understand perfectly well that the *last* day of the Christmas festivities finds one sated. One more party, and then thank God for

work. The mood is caught beautifully in II, iii, when Sir Toby wants
the party to go on while everyone else wants to go to bed. So the title
states a central dualism: a feast, an end to feasting. And, astonishingly, Barton illustrates the point through Maria.

Who is Maria? There's a question about her social position that is
functionally puzzling. She is some kind of companion. A younger
daughter of local gentry? Is she in Olivia's household to get married,
or because she has failed to get married? Does she rank with the
servants or the great family? Evidently, she's on the blurred edge of
the class-lines, above and below Malvolio. When Cesario puts the boot
in ('No, good swabber, I am to hull here a little longer') Maria has no
answer to the social insult. She is usually cast as a soubrette, pert and
bouncy. Barton made her an elderly spinster. (First Brenda Bruce,
then Elizabeth Spriggs.) This Maria 'is ageing, left on the shelf; she
waits desperately for the word from him, and what she often gets is a
dusty answer. The words " 'Tis too late to go to bed, now" are spoken
to her.'[21] Sir Toby, a well-born failure, is intelligent enough to be
aware of his own parasitism. But he is Maria's last chance. So there's
an elegiac quality at the heart of even the comic action.

The act of presentation of this *Twelfth Night* was genuinely original.
The 1971 revival had it perfectly gauged. The audience takes its seats
to find Richard Pasco's Orsino listening to his musicians. Presently an
aural disturbance comes upon the music. It grows louder, and is
identified as the sound of the sea crashing upon the shore. This sea is
the background to the action; it enters into the imagery of Orsino's
opening speech ('Receiveth as the sea') and intermittently returns to
the audience's consciousness. The sea implies a sense of the canon's
unity. It intimates that *Twelfth Night* is the beginning of the long swell
that culminates, beyond the breakers of the tragedies, in the final
romances. This *Twelfth Night* understands, and is aware of, *The
Tempest*. For Richard David, 'the sound of the sea reverberating
through key moments in the play' served 'to remind us of that sense of
the changes and chances of life that is surely intrinsic in the mood of
the play as in its basic situations'.[22] Robert Speaight had experienced a
sharper sense of 'the howling of the gale outside the gilded cage of
Orsino's palace; reality at odds with romanticism. . . .'[23] It is a
metamorphosis of that calm untroubled seascape that Daly provided
for the New Yorkers of 1894.

III

John Barton's *Twelfth Night* is the classic of recent times, and its statement, though modulated in later productions, has not, I think, been seriously challenged since. Basically, he takes the action seriously. From that perspective endless variations remain possible. Take the relationship between Sir Toby and Sir Andrew. It is, on Sir Toby's part, contemptuous and exploitative. And it ends in the unequivocal 'Will *you* help? An ass-head and a coxcomb and a knave, a thin-faced knave, a gull?' Now, how far is the director prepared to go in acknowledging the truth of this transaction? In the old days, no problem: Sir Andrew simply looked shocked at Sir Toby saying such *terrible* things. In the Regent's Park production of 1972, Sir Andrew stood stock-still for a long second, head bowed, as one pondering an irrevocable decision. He then marched off like an automaton, stage *left*, casting no glance at Sir Toby. Sir Toby limped off stage *right*. The audience could have no doubt that the friendship was permanently shattered.

Illusion, clearly, is what the director now perceives in this network of relationships. The concept became an emblem in Peter Gill's RSC production of 1974. The figure of a golden Narcissus hangs over the stage, the only pictorial element in a bleak box. The programme cites, of all people, R. D. Laing:

Narcissus fell in love with his image, taking it to be another. . . .

Jill is a distorting mirror to herself.
Jill has to distort herself to appear undistorted to herself.
To undistort herself, she finds Jack to distort her distorted image in his distorting mirror.
She hopes that his distortion of her distortion may undistort her image without her having to distort herself.

The atmosphere is vibrant with erotic undertones. Orsino's bisexuality is marked, and at least one critic had no doubt that Orsino was ready to grope the nearest, any time.[24] A boyish Viola (Jane Lapotaire) contributes to the general sexual confusion. Maria's maturity has become an RSC orthodoxy; Sir Toby is a gentleman, and intelligent – a decision that invariably imparts a stereoscopic depth to his scenes. David Waller has since explained, in interview, that his reading of the part is based on 'I hate a drunken rogue'. 'And it seems quite clear to me that he's referring quite consciously to himself.'[25]

The bleaker elements were intensified in this *Twelfth Night*. Barton had allowed himself a Feste with a certain Celtic charm (Emrys James), but Gill's Feste, Ron Pember, 'hinted always at a radical's social distaste for the antics of privilege. . . . He was discomforting, an outsider, almost malevolently saturnine, defying the sentimental response to Malvolio's plight by pressing home his final accusations with heartless accuracy in Act V. . . . Pember sang his songs with the gritty voice of the modern unaccompanied folk-singer.'26 There's more than a hint of Brecht in this. But there could in any case be no question of minimizing the effect of the final scene, given the major casting decision of this production: Nicol Williamson's Malvolio.

Nicol Williamson's salient characteristic is his capacity to portray pain. It is of a voltage that sets him apart from any other actor on the English stage. Not that his Malvolio was unfunny. His accent – which critics varied in finding Welsh, Scots, and veering from one to the other – placed him in the Baptist–Presbyterian tradition of the intolerant Nonconformist preacher on the make. More subtly, it placed him as an outsider (Illyria is set in the effete South of England). This Malvolio took his chances superbly in the garden scene, but his final humiliation was shattering. Michael Billington's verdict is precise: 'But what Williamson does so brilliantly is to blend high comedy and deep emotional pain . . . he tears Maria's epistle into minuscule fragments before departing to his own permanent, private hell, all dignity destroyed.'27 Williamson seems to have experimented with his final line during the production. When I saw it, the line was inaudible, spoken through the hands covering the face. Robert Speaight writes of a 'fourfold repetition'.28 The wound is open, and Orsino cannot heal it. The shock waves travel back through the entire action.

IV

Narcissism, eroticism and alienation, illusion ending in anguish: is this the last word of the current era on *Twelfth Night*? I don't think so; it appears to me rather as an overcompensation, an emphatic rejection of a stage cliché that had hardened into a lie. The modern statement on *Twelfth Night* has its textual justification: one has to ignore a great deal to build a production around the celebration of cakes and ale. And the play has to respond to certain tendencies of our own era. To cite a few, a taste for dark comedy has long been prevalent. The most influential (upon the stage) of recent Shakespearean writers, Jan Kott, treated *Twelfth Night* in a chapter entitled 'Shakespeare's bitter Arcadia'.[29] Moreover, the Problem Plays have, so to speak, territorially expanded. *Measure for Measure* and *Troilus and Cressida* are played far more often than ever before, and they now look like mainstream Shakespeare, not aberrations.[30] Then again, we ought not to ignore the oblique impact of Chekhov.

I earlier cited Trevor Nunn's identification of the 'Chekhov-like centre' of the play, and the point is worth pursuing. One often uses the word 'chekhovian' loosely, to indicate an autumnal atmosphere surrounding agreeable but rather futile people discussing, in an aimless way, what to do next. The word tends to drift away from its moorings. 'Chekhovian' means *like Chekhov*, and his importance on today's stage goes beyond his actual productions. Quite often one sees a *Twelfth Night* with II, iii, played as a homage to Chekhov: the sense of lateness and futility, the pauses, the alternation of manic gaiety and brooding, the inconsequentiality and missed connections:

> *Sir Toby:* Does not our lives consist of the four elements?
> *Sir Andrew:* Faith, so they say: but I think it rather consists of eating and drinking.
> *Sir Toby:* Th'art a scholar; let us therefore eat and drink.

The scene – it occurs in Olivia's household but comes over as a tavern scene – reminds us of the tavern scene in *2 Henry IV*, as the old Falstaff fondles Doll Tearsheet – 'do not bid me remember mine end' – and recalls the RSC's Chekhov-oriented production of the mid-sixties. (I think it true that contemporary taste prefers the second part of *Henry IV* to the first; and this used not to be so.) It is not in question that Chekhov is the father of Beckett and Pinter; he is important today in a way that Ibsen is not. Not everyone will go all the way with Christopher Booker's judgement: 'It is for our recognition of this melancholy, arid picture that I believe we have quietly elevated Chekhov into the supreme "serious" playwright of our age.'[31] We have none the less to acknowledge him as an unseen presence in the world of comedy. Through him, one catches at the implications of 'autumnal'. The subtext of autumn is winter: and one wonders if winter is not after all the right season for a setting of *Twelfth Night*.[32]

Chekhov, if you like, is a surface presence. But there is an underground subsidence that affects even more our view of *Twelfth Night*. The practical joke has vanished. I don't mean that it has ceased to exist; but its sanctions have. Our ancestors, as the memoirs testify, took a robust pleasure in practical jokes. The fondness for them persisted through the nineteenth century. In the last generation or so, the relish for them has ebbed away. As I take it, we know too much about the sadistic undercurrent of much practical joking to be at ease with it. It is one of the social changes of our lifetime that the historian should learn to document. Its passing means that the entire network of assumptions sustaining the old *Twelfth Night* has collapsed. And that raises the whole question of what is called, for want of a better word, comedy. The theory of comedy is the search for a better word. Perhaps all theoreticians of comedy should take their lead from Aristotle, who passed up the opportunity of making up his lecture-notes into a book, opting for the easier field of tragedy. His reviews have probably gained from that heroic evasion. A modern production of *Twelfth Night* is obliged to redefine comedy, knowing always that its ultimate event is the destruction of a notably charmless bureaucrat. There it is, and it happens. Do we laugh at it?

Twelfth Night, which appears as a machine for inducing laughter, discloses itself in the end as a machine for suppressing it. One is always aware of mixed responses in the theatre, of laughter in the wrong places. It's a general hazard of playgoing, and one accepts it without comment. But once, at a repertory production under a man who knew his business, I understood it as the dramatist's design: what had seemed an imperfection of theatre experience became the truth of the play. Malvolio's entrance in Act V created a storm of laughter. The interventions of Fabian and Feste, and the dawning awareness of Olivia, became the implacable advance of a reality that stifled laughter. The laughter of others, but not of oneself, became the experience of the drama. One by one the laughs ceased, like lights going out in the house, as the edge of the great play, dark as logic, moved over the consciousness of the audience. It received in total silence the destruction of Malvolio, and the strained half-moment that followed 'I'll be revenged on the whole pack of you' bore the meaning of the play. That silence, that end of laughter, is today's *Twelfth Night*.

NOTES

1   G. C. D. Odell, *Shakespeare from Betterton to Irving*, 2 vols (New York: Scribner, 1920), Vol. I, p. 442.
2   28 November 1894. Cited in John Russell Brown, *Shakespeare's Plays in Performance* (Harmondsworth: Penguin, 1969), p. 244.
3   Augustin Daly, New York, 1869. The prompt-book for this production is now lodged at the Folger Shakespeare Library, Washington, DC. In this and the next five notes I give the Folger call-mark for the prompt-book: TN, 9.
4   Adelaide Neilson, London, 1878. Folger: TN, 18.
5   Ibid.
6   Folger: TN, 30.

7   Neilson: TN, 18.

8   Henry Irving, London, 1884. Folger: TN, 13.

9   See John Elsom, *Postwar British Theatre* (London: Routledge & Kegan Paul, 1976), pp. 72–7; and John Russell Taylor, *Anger and After* (Harmondsworth: Penguin, 1963), pp. 28–37.

10   The phrase is Kenneth Tynan's. I take it from his review of a 1948 production, reprinted in his *A View of the English Stage* (Frogmore, St Albans: Paladin, 1976), p. 70.

11   J. L. Styan, *The Shakespeare Revolution: Criticism and Performance in the Twentieth Century* (Cambridge: Cambridge University Press, 1977), p. 95. Granville-Barker's *Twelfth Night* is discussed at length, pp. 90–5.

12   John Barton has said: 'I issued a caveat to the cast at the start of rehearsals against "business", – *Twelfth Night* seems to have a tendency to accrue excessive business at many points.' Quoted in Stanley Wells, *Royal Shakespeare: Four Major Productions at Stratford-upon-Avon* (Manchester: Manchester University Press, 1977), p. 45.

13   Laurence Kitchin, *Mid-Century Drama* (London: Faber, 1960), p. 45.

14   *Shakespeare Quarterly*, vol. IX (1958), pp. 523–4.

15   Ibid., vol. XII (1961), p. 427. This relates to the 1960 revival.

16   See Ralph Berry, *On Directing Shakespeare: Interviews with Contemporary Directors* (London and New York: Croom Helm and Barnes & Noble, 1977), p. 60.

17   'Some gaiety is lost,' felt Rosemary Anne Sissons in the *Stratford-upon-Avon Herald*, 25 April 1958.

18   Robert Speaight, 'The 1960 season at Stratford-upon-Avon', *Shakespeare Quarterly*, vol. XI (1960), p. 450.

19   For two admirable discussions of the casting options, see Brown, op. cit., pp. 222–8: and A. C. Sprague and J. C. Trewin, *Shakespeare's Plays Today: Some Customs and Conventions of the Stage* (Columbia, SC: University of South Carolina Press, 1970), pp. 92–7.

20   The production is discussed very fully in Wells, op. cit., pp. 43–63.

21   Gareth Lloyd Evans, 'Interpretation or experience? Shakespeare at Stratford', *Shakespeare Survey 23* (1970), p. 135.

22   Richard David, 'Of an age and for all time: Shakespeare at Stratford', *Shakespeare Survey 25* (1972), p. 167.

23   Robert Speaight, 'Shakespeare in Britain', *Shakespeare Quarterly*, vol. XX (1969), p. 439.

24   B. A. Young, *The Financial Times*, 23 August 1974.

25   Quoted by Peter Thomson, in 'The smallest season: the Royal Shakespeare Company at Stratford in 1974', *Shakespeare Survey 28* (1975), p. 145.

26   Ibid., pp. 145–6.

27   *The Guardian*, 23 August 1974.

28   Robert Speaight, 'Shakespeare in Britain, 1974', *Shakespeare Quarterly*, vol. XXV (1974), p. 392.

29   Jan Kott, *Shakespeare Our Contemporary*, 2nd ed. (London: Methuen, 1967).

30   A discussion of the 'problem play' category ought, in my view, to begin with *The Merchant of Venice* before continuing with *Twelfth Night*.

31   Christopher Booker, 'Mirror of our melancholy', *Daily Telegraph*, 26 February 1977.

32   Winter, in fact, was the setting for Terry Hands' production (RSC, 1979–80).

Index

Addenbrooke, David 16, 107
Adrian, Max 113
Alma-Tadema, Sir Lawrence 24, 35
Alvarez, A. 57, 64
Andrews, Harry 39
Annis, Francesca 61, 64
Ansorge, Peter 36, 48
Arden, John 76–7
Ardrey, Robert 31
Asche, Oscar 23
Atienza, Edward 51
Atkinson, Brooks 71, 82
Aylmer, Felix 69

Baily, James 89
Bartholomeusz, Dennis 15
Barton, Anne 41
Barton, John 4, 7, 31, 40–1, 44–5,
  50–1, 56–63, 74, 82, 113, 115, 119
Battenhouse, Roy 81
Beauman, Sally 82
Beckerman, Bernard 13, 16–17
Beckett, Samuel 13, 117
Benson, Sir Frank Robert 23–4, 34
Benthall, Michael 70–1, 87, 89
Berry, Ralph 36, 106, 119
Bevington, David 37
Billington, Michael 116
Bland, Marjorie 46
Blatchley, John 39
Booker, Christopher 3, 16, 117, 119
Brecht, Bertolt, 11, 30, 36, 116
Brien, Alan 31, 36, 57, 82
Brown, John Russell 8–9, 16, 76, 82,
  86, 106
Brook, Peter 4, 6, 8–9, 12–13, 16,
  38–9, 45, 47
Bryden, Ronald 31, 76, 99–100, 107
Buckingham, Duke of (John
  Sheffield) 34

Burge, Stuart 46
Bury, John 7–8, 75, 98–9
Bruce, Brenda 114
Burton, Richard 70–1
Byrne, Muriel St Clare 91, 93, 106,
  112

Calder-Marshall, Anna 46
Chekhov, A. P. 117
Church, Tony 61
Cibber, Theophilus 34
Cocteau, Jean 52
Cohn, Ruby 35–6
Coleridge, S. T. 84
Congreve, William, 113
Cook, Judith 16
Coward, Noel 4
Craig, Hardin 47
Crick, Bernard 105, 108
Cushman, Robert 108

Daly, Augustin 14, 109, 111, 114, 118
David, Richard 36, 38, 53, 55, 64,
  67, 81, 114, 119
Dennis, John 19
Dickins, R. 23–4, 29, 35
Dionisotti, Paola 46
Dostoevsky, F. 12
Durgnat, Raymond 67, 81
Dyck, Sir Anthony van 112
Dylan, Bob 100

Eder, Richard 65
Edinborough, Arnold 47, 82
Eisenstein, S. 68
Elgar, Sir Edward 113
Elliott, Michael 39
Elsom, John 3, 7, 16, 61, 64, 85, 106,
  108, 119
Emerson, Sally 64

Empson, William 41, 48, 63, 65
Erlich, Avi 108
Evans, Gareth Lloyd 76, 82, 119
Evans, Oliver H. 63
Eyre, Richard 108

Farrah 78
Finney, Albert 85–6, 105
Fleming, Tom 39
Forbes-Robertson, Sir Johnston 85–6
Ford, John 32
Forrest, Edwin 23
Fox, Edward 85
Freud, Sigmund 43
Furness, H. H. 35

Garrett, George P. 81
Garrett, John 106
Garrick, David 1
Gascoigne, Bamber 82
Geduld, Harry M. 68, 81
Gelfman, Jane R. 81
Gellert, Roger 40, 47, 95, 106–7
Genest, John 34
Genet, Jean 59
Genn, Leo 69
Gentleman, Francis 65
Gielgud, Sir John 6, 84, 86, 89, 93, 106, 112
Giles, David 40, 47
Gill, Peter 115–16
Goddard, Harold C. 72, 81
Gould, Gerald 66, 81
Granville-Barker, Harley 112, 119
Grass, Günter 30, 36
Griffiths, Richard 46
Guthrie, Sir Tyrone 29, 40, 50, 53–5, 67
Gwilym, Mike 64

Habicht, Werner 108
Hack, Keith 42, 44–5, 50–1, 61–2
Hall, Sir Peter 4, 6–8, 10, 16, 28, 50–1, 56–8, 62, 74–5, 82, 85, 90, 95–8, 101, 105, 107, 112–13
Hamilton, A. C. 47–8
Hands, Terry 4, 33, 77–80, 82, 119

Hardison, O. B. 81
Harris, Rosemary 95
Harvey, Gabriel 84
Harvey, Laurence 52
Hazlitt, William 20–1, 66, 72, 81
Heeley, Desmond 94
Helpmann, Robert 69, 87, 89–90
Henry, Martha 44
Hill, Aaron 34
Hilliard, Nicholas 76
Hobson, Sir Harold 95, 106
Hogarth, William 1
Hogg, Ian 32
Holinshed, Raphael 77
Holm, Ian 75
Honigmann, E. A. J. 15
Hope-Wallace, Philip 36
Hosley, Richard 81
Houtchens, C. W. 35
Houtchens, L. H. 35
Howard, Alan 33, 59, 77, 79–80, 82–3, 85, 101, 103–4
Howe, P. P. 35
Hunt, Holman 1
Hunt, Hugh 113
Hunt, Leigh 20, 22
Hurren, Kenneth 64
Hutt, William 43, 73

Ibsen, Henrik 117
Ingham, Barrie 43
Inglis, Brian 64
Innes, Christopher 36
Irving, Sir Henry 23–5, 34–5, 111, 119

Jacobi, Derek 105
James, Emrys 79, 116
Jamieson, Michael 47
Jewett, Henry 110–11
Jones, D. A. N. 64, 103, 107
Jones, Ernest 89
Jorgens, Jack J. 81
Jorgensen, Paul A. 81

Kay, Charles 76
Kean, Edmund 21, 24

Kemble, John Philip 19–22, 24, 33, 63, 65, 93
Kenny, Sean 95
King, Francis 108
Kitchin, Laurence 28, 35, 81, 112, 119
Knight, G. Wilson 36, 38, 87
Kott, Jan 13, 17, 57, 75, 98, 116, 119
Kozintsev, Grigori 12–13, 17, 86
Kyle, Barry 46

Laing, R. D. 107, 115
Landau, Jack 50
Langham, Michael 71–4, 76
Lapotaire, Jane 115
Lawrence, Sir Thomas 93
Leech, Clifford 16
Leggatt, Alexander 4
Levin, Bernard 3, 16
Lewis, Peter 36
Lewsen, Charles 48
Lloyd, Bernard 46
Locke, Philip 51
Loftis, John 34
Lonsdale, Frederick 113

McEwan, Geraldine 113
McGlinchee, Claire, 64
Machiavelli, Niccolo 98
McInnerny, Tim 62
McKellen, Ian 29
McKern, Leo 51, 53
Macready, W. C. 22–3, 34–5
Mairowitz, David Zane 64
Marcus, Frank 64, 107
Margeson, J. M. R. 16
Marowitz, Charles 16
Maugham, Somerset 113
Maxwell, James 39
Miles, Sir Bernard 71
Miller, Jonathan 3–4, 9, 16, 43, 45, 48, 93, 97
Monette, Richard 106
Montaigne, Michel de 98
Morgann, Maurice 3
Morley, Christopher 102–3
Morley, Henry 35
Morley, Sheridan 16

Moshinsky, Elijah 50–1
Muir, Kenneth 11, 16

Neilson, Adelaide 111, 118–19
Neville, John 29, 71, 88
Newlin, Jeanne T. 65
Nicholls, Anthony 39
Nightingale, Benedict 33, 36, 49, 57, 59, 63–4, 80, 82–3, 104, 107
Nobili, Lila de 7, 113
Norton, Elliot 82
Nunn, Trevor 3–4, 7, 32, 101–2, 104, 113

O'Conor, Joseph 44
Odell, G. C. D. 34–5, 118
Olivier, Lord 1, 3, 6, 67–71, 75–6, 78, 80, 86, 92, 94–5, 112
Osborne, John, 3, 26, 30
O'Toole, Peter 6, 94–5

Palmer, John 26, 34–5, 72, 81
Papp, Joseph 17, 49, 63
Pascal, Blaise 98
Pasco, Richard 114
Pember, Ron 116
Pennell, Nicholas 106
Pennington, Michael 46
Pettigrew, John 73–4, 82
Phelps, Samuel 22–3
Phillips, Ambrose 34
Phillips, Robin 9, 17, 43–5, 105–6
Piachaud, R. -L. 26, 35
Pinter, Harold 32, 87, 116
Pirandello, Luigi 92
Plummer, Christopher 71–2
Porter, Eric 57, 76, 113
Price, Joseph G. 16, 47, 65
Priestley, J.B. 4
Pryce, Jonathan 108
Pryce-Jones, David 82, 107

Quayle, Anthony 27, 39, 52
Quilley, Denis 105
Quinn, Michael 81

Rain, Douglas 72–3
Raine, Craig 48

Rattigan, Sir Terence 3
Redgrave, Sir Michael 90–3
Richardson, Ian 31, 76
Robbins, John Franklyn 40
Roberts, Peter 81
Robertson, Toby 105
Rodway, Norman 59
Rogers, Paul 54
Rosenberg, Marvin 15

Scofield, Paul 12, 14, 84, 87, 89–90, 93
Shattuck, Charles H. 14–15, 17
Shaw, George Bernard 28, 52, 66
Shaw, Glen Byam 6, 27, 52, 54, 90
Sheridan, Thomas 19
Shulman, Milton 82
Sissons, Rosemary Anne 119
Smith, Derek 83
Speaight, Robert 7, 16, 41, 44, 48, 56–9, 64, 75, 82, 98–100, 102–3, 106–7, 112, 114, 116, 119
Spencer, Hazelton 34
Sprague, A. C. 16, 47, 66, 81, 119
Spriggs, Elizabeth 114
Spurling, Hilary 60, 64, 82, 107
Stavisky, S. A. 14, 25–6, 35
Stoppard, Tom 87
Stothard, Peter 48
Styan, J. L. 15-16
Symons, Arthur 24, 35

Tate, Nahum 19, 34
Taylor, John Russell 119
Terry, Ellen 35
Theobald, Lewis 34
Thomson, James 19
Thomson, Peter 48, 119
Tillyard, E. M. W. 11, 41, 48, 51, 63

Trewin, J. C. 15-16, 33, 36, 46–8, 56–7, 63–4, 71, 81, 89, 95, 97, 99–100, 103, 106–7, 119
Truman, Ralph 69
Tynan, Kenneth 12, 17, 27–8, 35, 81, 85, 119

Ustinov, Peter 17

Voth, Grant L. 63

Waller, David 105, 115
Walton, Sir William 70
Wardle, Irving 31, 33, 43, 46, 48, 64, 78, 80, 82–3, 105, 107–8
Warner, David 85–6, 95, 97–101, 107–8
Webster, Margaret 39
Weil, Herbert 38, 47
Wells, Stanley 5, 16, 107
West, Timothy 105
Wildgruber, Ulrich 108
Williams, Clifford 74
Williams, Michael 60
Williamson, Jane 39–40, 44, 47
Williamson, Nicol 32–3, 85, 116
Wilson, Edwin 35, 81
Wilson, John Dover 34–5, 54, 64
Wilton, Penelope 45
Wolfit, Sir Donald 5
Wood, John (actor) 3
Wood, John (director) 51, 65
Worsley, T. C. 55, 64, 92, 106
Wymark, Patrick 113

Yarvet, Yuri 12
Yoder, R. A. 63
Young, B. A. 36, 119